THOM BROOKS

REFORMING THE UK'S CITIZENSHIP TEST

Building Bridges, Not Barriers

BRISTOL
UNIVERSITY
PRESS

First published in Great Britain in 2022 by

Bristol University Press
University of Bristol
1–9 Old Park Hill
Bristol
BS2 8BB
UK
t: +44 (0)117 374 6645
e: bup-info@bristol.ac.uk

Details of international sales and distribution partners are available at
bristoluniversitypress.co.uk

British Library Cataloguing in Publication Data
A catalogue record for this book is available from the British Library

ISBN 978-1-5292-1852-7 hardcover
ISBN 978-1-5292-1853-4 ePub
ISBN 978-1-5292-1854-1 ePdf

Cover design: blu inc
Front cover image: Ian Taylor – unsplash.com

For Bhikhu Parekh

Contents

About the Author

Thom Brooks is Dean of Durham Law School and Professor of Law and Government at Durham University. He has held visiting appointments at Columbia, Harvard, Luiss, Nice, New York University, Oxford, Penn, St Andrews, Uppsala and Yale. His books include *Becoming British: UK Citizenship Examined* (Biteback 2016) and (ed) *Ethical Citizenship* (Palgrave 2014). He has published articles in *Criminal Law and Philosophy*; *Criminal Justice Ethics*; *Ethics*; *Ethics, Policy and Environment*; *European Human Rights Law Review*; *Harvard Review of Philosophy*; *Journal of Applied Philosophy*; *Journal of Criminal Law*; *Journal of Moral Philosophy*; *Journal of Social Philosophy*; *Modern Law Review*; *Netherlands Quarterly of Human Rights*; *New Criminal Law Review*; *The Good Society* and *Utilitas* among others. Since 2014, Brooks has advised the UK Labour Party on immigration law and policy and is Director of the Labour Academic Network creating a team of academic experts to support Labour's work in Parliament.

Preface

My biggest surprise in becoming a British citizen was how few citizens were aware of the UK's citizenship test, or able to pass it when asked questions from the official handbook. I stumbled on the test in 2009 when completing my application for an 'Indefinite Leave to Remain' visa which would permit me to keep my job and continue to live permanently in the UK. Working through the application, I saw a mysterious box asking me to confirm whether I had passed the test or taken an English language course that taught citizenship. Either way, I was required to show a pass certificate I did not have for a test that I did not know existed. Most people I spoke to who were born British did not know about the test and, if they did, had no idea what was in it.

Like so many others before me, I found a practice online citizenship test and promptly failed it. I picked up a test handbook and began studying in earnest as I had only weeks to pass it before my visa expired. When my students would come to my office at university to ask me a question, I would insist that I ask them a question first from the test handbook. I could not understand why so many enormously talented students at a leading Russell Group university studying law or politics – many of whom with an 'A*' or 'A' A-level grades in Politics – could get so many questions wrong. It was this that had first raised my suspicions about whether there was ever a consultation on the test before or after its launch, whether the information tested was genuinely essential to active citizenship and whether, in fact, all the facts included were even correct.

I have made some shocking findings, detailed in full for the first time here. While over two million have sat the test, there has never been any official review and continuing problems were either unchecked or ignored. Despite all main political parties claiming immigration was a priority issue, the citizenship test and its problems were rarely on their political radars. Otherwise, someone else would have drawn attention to what has become shocking: a British citizenship test for migrants that few British citizens can pass, with too little relevance to learning about making an active contribution as a permanent resident or citizen.

While making my initial discoveries, I found to my surprise that no one had published a report about the uses of these tests – which is still the only comprehensive report focused on the test across its three editions – and so I went ahead and did this on 13 June 2013. My report was covered by over 300 different media outlets around the world and the launch video has been viewed over 27,000 times, one of Durham University's most viewed lectures.[1] It has been the subject of Parliamentary debates and irked successive government ministers. But much more has happened in the nearly ten years since this first report, not least Brexit and a changing immigration system. There is a need for a clear, comprehensive and updated analysis of why there is a UK citizenship test, how it is intended to fulfil its aims and purposes, the evidence for whether these are achieved and with recommendations for how to improve the test – and the timing could not be more critical as the government is currently planning a new fourth edition that could appear as early as 2022.[2]

This book aims to fill the gap. It goes much further than my original report to analyse context, the contents of successive tests and the lessons that we can learn from elsewhere. I will argue that we make a choice between building bridges that

---

[1] Thom Brooks, 'The "Life in the UK" citizenship test: is it unfit for purpose?', Durham University, YouTube (18 June 2013).

[2] This book expands greatly on both my original citizenship test report and *Becoming British*. See Thom Brooks, *The 'Life in the United Kingdom' Citizenship Test: Is It Unfit for Purpose?* (Durham: Durham University, 2013) and Thom Brooks, *Becoming British: UK Citizenship Examined* (London: Biteback, 2016).

bring together citizens old and new or building barriers that are more easily created without introducing a test. This requires a shift away from Australia – a source of immigration policy ideas for both Labour and Conservative governments alike – to the United States which launched a test before either the UK or Australia.

I owe thanks to a great many people, including Diane Abbott, Orkun Akseli, Hilary Benn, Tony Blair, David Blunkett, Graham Brady, Gordon Brown, Robert Buckland, Liam Byrne, Alan Campbell, Matt Cavanagh, (Baroness) Shami Chakrabarti, Simon Child, Charles Clarke, Melanie Cooke, Yvette Cooper, Jeremy Corbyn, Alberto Costa, Gareth Dant, Don Flynn, Fabian Freyenhagen, Ged Grebby, Kate Green, David Hanson, Andrew Harrop, the late David Held, Peter Jones, Sunder Katwala, (Lord) Roy Kennedy, Holly Lynch, Harley Miller, David Miliband, Ed Miliband, David Miller, Tariq Modood, Richard Mullender, Kate Murray, Martin Nickson, (Baroness) Onora O'Neill, David Owen, Bridget Phillipson, Laura Pidcock, Devyani Prabhat, Erika Rackley, Harvey Redgrave, Rachel Reeves, Jonathan Reynolds, Bell Ribeiro-Addy, Martin Ruhs, Robert Schütze, Mathias Siems, Avital Simhony, James Simpson, (Baroness) Angela Smith, Jacqui Smith, Sonia Sodha, Marc Stears, Lachlan Stuart, Jason Sugarman, Luke Sullivan, Nick Thomas-Symonds, Jessica Toale, Anna Turley, Chuka Umunna, Astrid von Busekist, (Lord) William Wallace, Patrick Weil, Clare Williams, Phil Wilson and Phil Woolas. I am grateful to Kay Burley, Alfie Joey, Anna Jones and Anne Nyberg for especially interesting conversations about the test in interviews. I am further grateful to an anonymous reviewer who made several superb observations that further enriched this book.

My special thanks to Chi Onwurah, who was the first Member of Parliament to take an interest in this work and press for changes to the test and to (Lord) Roger Roberts of Llandudno who endorsed my original report and spoke at its launch. My thanks to my union UNISON and Show Racism the Red Card for regular invitations to speak about the test and related immigration issues. I have spoken regularly with (Baroness) Angela Smith and (Lord) Richard Rosser on this and related topics for many years, always wiser afterwards. I am enormously grateful to former Shadow Immigration Minister and close friend Afzal Khan for several fascinating discussions over the years. My thanks also to his predecessor Keir Starmer for insightful conversations about immigration law and policy and how it can become much improved. I benefited from discussing ideas in this book as part of Martha Nussbaum's 'Legal Philosophy Workshop' when visiting the University of Chicago Law School shortly before the UK's national lockdown in 2020. An earlier version of one of the chapters was presented at the University of Bristol's Centre for the Study of Ethnicity and Citizenship seminar. I am also grateful for the opportunity to present my original findings with the Tribune group of Labour MPs in October 2021.

My thanks to my family for their constant support. My wife Claire attended my citizenship ceremony and we still laugh at how 'It's Just the Bare Necessities' was sung as entertainment to welcome new citizens like me not least after paying the high fees to get there. While my young daughter Eve will never need to pass a test to be British like I did, my hope is that any future test is one that anyone in her generation would be able to pass and find a useful bridge connecting all citizens old and new.

I dedicate this book to one of my dearest friends, my mentor and guru for close to 20 years, Professor the Lord (Bhikhu) Parekh FBA. My intellectual debt to him and his extensive work is profound. I dedicate this book to him with my greatest thanks and deep admiration.

ONE

A Bad Pub Quiz

This book is about a test. The 'Life in the UK' citizenship test contains 24 multiple-choice questions to be answered over 45 minutes.[1] Applicants must score at least 75 per cent in getting 18 or more correct answers to pass. The test costs £50 and may be re-sat no more than once every seven days until passed.[2] Its original aim and purpose was to test an individual's ability to 'integrate and to become active citizens' with 'a level of knowledge about what it means to be a citizen of modern, democratic Britain'.[3]

The citizenship test *matters*. Since its launch on 1 November 2005, it has become a requirement for anyone applying for British citizenship – and for 'Indefinite Leave to Remain' permanent residency since 2007 as well.[4] Over two million

---

[1] See HM Government, 'Life in the UK test'. There is guidance on the identification required for taking the test and . See UK Visas and Immigration, 'Life in the UK test: identification documents' and PSI e-Assessment, 'Terms and conditions for booking and taking the Life in the UK test'.

[2] The test was £32.24 payable in exact change only on the day when I sat the test in 2009. It is now paid only online when booking a test.

[3] See David Blunkett MP, 'Preface' in Home Office, *Life in the United Kingdom: A Journey to Citizenship* (London: The Stationery Office, 2005): 4.

[4] There are several exceptions, for example for individuals aged under 18 or over 65 years old, or for anyone with long-term physical or mental conditions. See HM Government, 'Life in the UK test' and HM Government, 'Knowledge of language and Life in the UK exemption: long term physical or mental condition'.

tests have been taken since. While a second edition appeared in 2007 under New Labour, this was followed by a third in 2013 under the Tory-led coalition government and there has never been any official consultation or review to consider whether the test is fit for purpose or how well it has achieved its original aims.

This failure of successive governments to take sufficient time to put this together, fact-check information and keep the test handbook up to date has created serious problems that have gone on for too long unnoticed. In 2013, I published what was until this book the only comprehensive report about the 'Life in the UK' citizenship test across its three editions.[5] My report was the subject of several Parliamentary debates and received global media attention.[6]

What I uncovered was a rushed effort full of errors of fact, inconsistencies and omissions that has got worse after almost a decade later with no clear plan to correct these problems. This is an enormous challenge as it impacts on anyone considering applying for permanent residency or citizenship, and so there are potentially serious long-term consequences for how these individuals are affected – with implications for the kinds of citizens they become. The present risk is that the test does not ensure citizens have integrated, but instead leaves them feeling alienated and disengaged, which is deeply problematic for the UK's democratic health.

---

[5] See Brooks, The 'Life in the United Kingdom' Citizenship Test. See also Thom Brooks, 'Testing times for citizenship', Centre Wright (Summer 2016): 32 and Thom Brooks, 'The Life in the UK citizenship test and the urgent need for its reform' in Devyani Prabhat (ed), Citizenship in Times of Turmoil? Theory, Practice and Policy (London: Edward Elgar, 2019): 22–60.

[6] For a few examples, see Lord Roberts of Llandudno, House of Lords debate, 4 July 2013, column 1397; 'Immigration: UK citizenship and nationality', House of Lords debate, 10 October 2013, columns GC114–; Justin Parkinson, 'British citizenship test "like bad pub quiz"', BBC News (13 June 2013); Press Association, 'Citizenship test has become a bad pub quiz, says academic', The Guardian (14 June 2013).

The test's original purpose was to provide a means of ensuring new migrants had accepted British values and integrated, as will be explored in the next chapter. Yet, it is regularly lampooned as the test for British citizenship that few British citizens can pass. Instead of bringing citizens old and new together, there is troubling evidence that the test pushes them further apart, creating resentment among naturalized citizens for having to jump an unnecessary hurdle to prove sufficient knowledge about their adopted country that too few citizens can answer correctly and without any engagement since its launch with anyone who has passed the test to become British. The test bears all the trappings of a bureaucratic hurdle that has lost sight of, or an interest in, its original purpose. Like Kafka's *Trial*, the test creaks on, disinterested in how it might be reformed, improved and made more relevant.[7]

Let me outline what the government has not bothered to notice. The test handbook in use today contains errors of fact, such as claiming that the highest bank note in UK circulation is £50 despite there being a £100 bank note issued by the Bank of Scotland, RBS and Clydesdale Bank.[8] Or that Margaret Thatcher has died – the test handbook claims she remains alive.[9] The test is riddled with various inconsistencies: you do not need to know how many MPs sit in Parliament, but you do need to know the number of representatives in all regional assemblies; nor do you need to know there is a UK Supreme Court, but you do need to know about lesser courts.[10] The test fails to include lots of information that any citizen might

[7]   See Franz Kafka, *The Trial*, trans. Willa and Edwin Muir (New York: Schocken Books, 1992).

[8]   See Home Office, *Life in the United Kingdom: A Guide for New Residents, 3rd edition* (London: The Stationery Office, 2013): 74 (hereafter '*Third Edition*') and Gordon Blackstock, 'Scots immigrants left confused as UK citizenship test app gives incorrect answers', *Daily Record* (21 March 2021).

[9]   See Home Office, *Third Edition*, 67.

[10] Ibid, 129–132, 144–147.

be expected to know such as how to contact emergency services, report a crime, register with a GP or use the NHS. And then what the test handbook does include is often purely trivial, such as the approximate age of Big Ben's clock, the height of the London Eye and from which country was the wife of the founder of the UK's first curry house and that they had eloped.[11]

That's not all. There is a deep gender imbalance from cover to cover where women receive relatively rare attention. For example, the historical chapters give dates of birth for 29 men, but only four women.[12] And, finally, according to the government in response to my research, not all of the approximately 3,000 facts (including 278 historical dates) are actually on any test.[13] Instead, only some are tested but the government does not say which – and this is contrary to the guidance in the official handbook that all facts may be included on any test. In other words, the *official* view about the official guidance is it's not all factually true about what is on the test.

The British citizenship test is a test few British citizens can pass. It makes a mockery of the system for naturalization that applicants for citizenship must prove they possess a knowledge about 'life in the United Kingdom' sufficient for citizenship that most citizens do not appear, in fact, to possess. For example, one recent study by researchers at the University of Essex found that up to two-thirds of the public cannot pass the test.[14] There is no good reason to think passing it helps new citizens integrate better with established citizens who can't pass it.

---

[11] Ibid, 108, 113 and 42.

[12] Ibid, 14–69.

[13] See Lord Taylor of Holbeach, 'Immigration: UK citizenship and nationality', House of Lords debate, 10 October 2013, column GC128.

[14] See Rebecca Creed, 'Essex University: two thirds would not pass UK citizenship test', *Daily Gazette* (9 January 2021). As one interviewee told me, the citizenship test was "the worst test I've ever taken in my life – and I know a lot about being tested. I'm a PhD student".

It is alarming that this test – which is central to determining whether or not hundreds of thousands of people may become permanent residents or citizens – has been allowed to become overridden with such fundamental flaws in its design and execution with no serious interest in putting it right. In fact, most academic commentary about immigration and settlement makes little or no mention of it at all, too.[15] Nor do most studies about multiculturalism and integration mention these tests either – even though integrating migrants is part of the citizenship test's *raison d'être*.[16] In the Home Office's *A Practical*

---

[15] For example, see Nathan Akehurst, 'Why Labour must be the party of migration justice', *Renewal* 27(4) (2019): 23–34; Etienne Balibar, *Citizenship* (Cambridge: Polity, 2015); Christopher Bertram, *Do States Have the Right to Exclude Immigrants?* (Cambridge: Polity, 2018); Gillian Brock, *Migration and Political Theory* (Cambridge: Polity, 2021): 84–87; James Hampshire, *The Politics of Immigration* (London: Routledge, 2013): 125–127; Jonathan Portes, *What Do We Know and What Should We Do About Immigration?* (Thousand Oaks: SAGE, 2019); Alex Sager (ed), *The Ethics and Politics of Immigration: Core Issues and Emerging Trends* (London: Rowman & Littlefield, 2016); Rosemary Sales, *Understanding Immigration and Refugee Policy: Contradictions and Continuities* (Bristol: Policy Press, 2007); Sarah Spencer, *The Migration Debate* (Bristol: Policy Press, 2011); Christopher Heath Wellman, 'Immigration', *Stanford Encyclopedia of Philosophy* (21 May 2019); Colin Yeo, *Welcome to Britain: Fixing Our Broken Immigration System* (London: Biteback, 2020).

[16] For example, see Tom Farer, *Migration and Integration: The Case for Liberalism with Borders* (Cambridge: Cambridge University Press, 2020); David Goodhart, *The British Dream: Successes and Failures of Post-War Immigration* (London: Atlantic Books, 2013); Afua Hirsch, *Brit(ish): On Race, Identity and Belonging* (London: Jonathan Cape, 2018); Will Kymlicka, *Multicultural Odysseys: Navigating the New International Politics of Diversity* (Oxford: Oxford University Press, 2007); Alan Patten, *The Moral Foundations of Minority Rights* (Princeton: Princeton University Press, 2014); Anne Phillips, *Multiculturalism without Culture* (Princeton: Princeton University Press, 2007); Peter Ratcliffe and Ines Newman (eds), *Promoting Social Cohesion: Implications for Policy and Evaluation* (Bristol: Policy Press, 2011): 195–198.

Guide to Living in the United Kingdom, the guide makes reference to the test only once and briefly offers a link for readers to find out what it is.[17] If the Home Office is not much bothered, it sends a clear message that something has gone wrong.

The time is ripe for a rethink. The government has made clear its plans to produce a new fourth edition of the test handbook, as part of its plans for a new, post-Brexit immigration system.[18] We must revisit why the test is used in the first place, critically examine whether the test across its three different editions is achieving its aims and purposes, and we must be clear about how a new fourth edition of this test might succeed where other versions have fallen short, noting lessons from citizenship tests used elsewhere.

In this book, I will argue that the UK's citizenship test is in urgent need of reform and a relaunch.[19] I have described the test as 'like a bad quiz' that is unfit for purpose, but it is not only me that thinks that.[20] Even former Home Secretary, and now Health Secretary, Sajid Javid used my characterization to express his own concern with the test.[21] This cannot be allowed to continue unchanged.

---

[17] Home Office, *A Practical Guide to Living in the United Kingdom* (London: The Stationery Office (TSO), 2014): 13. See Thom Brooks, *A Practical Guide to Living in the United Kingdom: A Report* (Durham: Durham University, 2015).

[18] It is surprising to me to find the government still making up its mind in how to adjust the immigration system so long after Brexit. There would have been more certainty and less confusion if a coherent vision was worked out in advance.

[19] See Thom Brooks, 'The UK citizenship test is closer to a bad pub quiz than a rite of passage. It has to be re-written', *The Independent* (25 August 2020).

[20] See Mock the Week, 'The British citizenship test is like a bad pub quiz (and so is Mock the Week)', BBC 2 (10 January 2019).

[21] See Thom Brooks, 'Sajid Javid is right – the British citizenship test is like a bad pub quiz. So what is he going to do about it?' *The Independent* (3 October 2018).

For me, the UK's citizenship test is not a topic of mere academic study in Law or Political Science. One reason why I know its importance and how it has affected naturalized British citizens is for the simple fact that I had to sit and pass it in the process of my becoming British. A crucial concern of mine about studies of citizenship, immigration and integration is that too many involved in researching and writing in this area have not experienced this first-hand or had sufficient exposure to those who have. Too many voices about what to do about immigration matters are individuals who have no direct knowledge of immigrating themselves nor of those who have.

This failure to connect with how the system works first-hand is a problem. It leaves an unacknowledged gap between theory and practice unnoticed if only following a desk-based documentary trail. If someone has never had to fill in a citizenship application form, they might easily overlook what is required – such as passing the citizenship test – and the lived experience of doing so. I have filled in the form – passing the test in 2009 and earning my British citizenship in 2011. The importance of having such a *phenomenological* perspective – in possessing the experience from a first-person point of view – cannot be overstated.[22]

This book will draw on a combination of my in-depth research, semi-structured interviews with key figures behind the test's original creation, including former Home Secretaries, Immigration Ministers and their Shadows, a deep dive into Parliamentary records, and my first-hand knowledge of having taken the test.[23] These sources provide the fullest account to

---

[22] On phenomenological approaches, see David Woodruff Smith, 'Phenomenology', *Stanford Encyclopedia of Philosophy* (2013); W. Alex Edmonds and Thomas D. Kennedy, *An Applied Guide to Research Designs: Quantitative, Qualitative and Mixed Methods, 2nd edition* (Thousand Oaks: SAGE, 2017): chapter 14 ('phenomenological perspective').

[23] By 'their shadows', I refer to the positions of Shadow Home Secretary and Shadow Immigration Minister, a number of whom I have advised on Parliamentary written questions detailed in later chapters.

date of the intentions for the test, its design and help explain why its delivery has not met its anticipated expectations. My intention is to lay bare the test's problems as an ineffective and inconsistent *barrier*. However, my aims are not merely critical, but constructive: I will provide concrete recommendations for how this at present poor barrier to entry can be transformed into a long overdue *bridge* to citizenship fostering greater inclusion and integration.

Instead of bringing citizens old and new closer together, the UK's citizenship test has created a further sense of alienation for migrants who have come to see it as an unreasonable and unnecessary barrier to keep migrants out rather than a bridge for new citizens to cross, as will be shown in later chapters. With each edition of the test, it moves ever further away from its original purpose. This book is about explaining how this has happened – *and how to fix it*. It is my view that the citizenship test can and should play an important role, but only if it is fundamentally changed. The time is now.

TWO

Why Test for Citizenship?

Becoming a citizen does not have its traditional origins in passing any formal test.[1] This naturally raises the question: so why create and require a citizenship test today?

The UK's common law has always allowed the naturalization of foreign nationals, subject to various conditions. One of these is an oath of allegiance to the Crown and a second is possessing a satisfactory knowledge of English, among others.[2] These common law requirements were first put into statute through the British Nationality and Status of Aliens Act 1914. While the oath must be performed, there was no set test for knowledge and requirements centred around having residency over a set period while maintaining a 'good character'.[3] This was changed in the British Nationality Act 1981 which added the requirement that anyone applying for naturalization must have 'sufficient knowledge about life in the United Kingdom', but it did not specify how this was to be done.[4]

It was not until the Nationality, Immigration and Asylum Act 2002 that Parliament formally required that naturalizing citizens prove their knowledge of life in the UK by passing a

---

[1]   For an overview about theories of citizenship, see Thom Brooks, 'Citizenship' in Hugh LaFollette (ed), *The International Encyclopedia of Ethics* (Oxford: Blackwell, 2013): 764–773.

[2]   See Brooks, *Becoming British*, 23–52.

[3]   See s2 of the British Nationality and Status of Aliens Act 1914.

[4]   See Schedule 1 (Requirements for Naturalisation) 1(1)(ca) of British Nationality Act 1981.

test. However, this required a test to be put together which took a few years to develop. So, that's a brief *legal* history of the citizenship test's origins. But it does not explain why a requirement to have 'knowledge about life in the United Kingdom' became a mandatory multiple-choice test in force today.

Working through the records, the earliest mention in Parliament for having a citizenship test that I have found is by George Buchanan, a Labour MP representing Glasgow who had served in Clement Attlee's government as Under-Secretary of State for Scotland. In a 1935 speech earlier in his career, Buchanan said 'the test for naturalisation ought to be *a citizenship test*'. He argued that while various sons of immigrants living in his constituency were able to become British citizens after fighting in the First World War, their parents could not and such a pathway to naturalization should be made available to them.[5] There is nothing to suggest that Buchanan was advocating for a test sat like a school exam. No further mention of this proposal for a test was made in that 1935 debate or afterwards by him or anybody else for another 66 years.

The UK citizenship test's contemporary roots stem from 2001 events, but before 9/11. Former Immigration Minister Phil Woolas explained to me that the government had growing concerns about what were described as 'parallel communities'. These were areas that migrants had settled over the 20th century where standards of English fluency and economic activity were relatively low. The concern was that these were communities that had not fully integrated and operated separately like islands across the country. This isolation, combined with lack of opportunities, was thought to fuel a worrying level of alienation and discontent that might grow and could become worse.

---

[5] See George Buchanan, 'Home Office', House of Commons debate, 16 July 1935, column 995 (emphasis added).

These concerns came to the fore following the May 2001 riots in areas such as Burnley and Oldham (the latter was Woolas's constituency). These events were the trigger for Tony Blair's Labour government to start the engines in committing itself to launching new policies aimed at improving integration of migrants old and new with settled UK citizens. The terrorist attacks in New York on 9/11 (2001) and those in London on 7/7 (2005) only made the government more resolute to move forward; but, as Woolas described it to me, plans to act were already in place by the time of these events.

While the government was committed to act, those engaged in these discussions have told me that there was still a lack of clarity over what form these actions would take. One individual involved in that debate described it to me as a confusion over whether to steer immigration and citizenship policy by either "guilt or greed": a choice needed to be made between prioritizing the economic benefits or some other policy goal.

Either way, the government was in desperate need of a plan to implement swiftly. A convenient model was found in Australia, which had just completed a wide-ranging review of its citizenship policies with several significant changes. The UK could effectively look to piggyback on Australia's lead to expedite reform – and it did to some extent.

The Australian Citizenship Council launched its report *Australian Citizenship for a New Century*, led by Sir Ninian Stephen, in February 2000 after a public consultation.[6] In its official response to this report in May 2001, the Australian government committed itself to affirmation ceremonies to welcome new Australian citizens, eligible individuals were to be encouraged to become Australian citizens and the report supports applicants for citizenship being able to demonstrate knowledge of the responsibilities and privileges enjoyed on

---

[6] Australian Citizenship Council, *Australian Citizenship for a New Century* (Canberra: Australian Citizenship Council, 2000).

becoming a citizen.[7] This led to the launch of citizenship ceremonies and clarifying the application process for citizenship generally. Both ideas were later adopted by Blair's government shortly afterwards. The Australian government provided a model that would be replicated in the UK.

While Australia did not launch its own citizenship test in 2007, it nonetheless exercised a strong influence elsewhere. The review in Australia had already set out the backdrop that would help define the UK's approach. Specifically, the test would be aimed at ensuring a common bond of knowledge and values shared between citizens old and new, and it would play heed to and respect the multiculturalism within the society.

What was needed in the UK was its own review, taking inspiration primarily from the work done in Australia, of how and where to best forge these bonds of integration in Britain. These reviews would be shaped by the view that British citizenship is a shared sense of values like in Australia. But while the UK was influenced by the Australian approach, this idea of a values-led approach to citizenship is not an import.

The idea makes an early appearance a few weeks after the Australian report in a speech by Prime Minister Tony Blair in March 2000, known as 'Blair's Britain' speech.[8] He identified British values of 'fair play, creativity, tolerance and an outward-looking approach to the world'.[9] A shared British identity was found in these 'shared values not in unchanging institutions'.[10] Our shared values create a common British identity that has altered over time, or so it was argued. Blair stated: 'This nation has been formed by a particularly rich

---

[7] Australian Government, *Australian Citizenship ... A Common Bond: Government Response to the Report of the Australian Citizenship Council* (Canberra: Commonwealth of Australia, 2001): 13, 15 and 19.

[8] See Tony Blair, 'Tony Blair's Britain speech', *The Guardian* (28 March 2000).

[9] Ibid.

[10] Ibid.

complex of experiences: successive waves of invasion and immigration and trading partnerships, a potent mix of cultures and traditions which have flowed together to make us what we are today.'[11] Blair's avowed aim was to act to strengthen these British values for a 'new modern patriotism' making for a 'stronger and fairer' Britain.[12] These views set out in 2000 help set the tone for how a new citizenship test would be developed around shared values and what we all have in common, rather than a more exclusive or historically fixed conception of Britishness.

The first of three review groups was the Commission on the Future of Multi-Ethnic Britain, originally launched in 1998 by the Runnymede Trust.[13] Its chair, Bhikhu Parekh, now Lord Parekh of Kingston upon Hull, is one of the UK's most respected political theorists and a leading proponent of multiculturalism. The Commission's findings, published in October 2000 in what is known as 'the Parekh Report', rejected the view of Britain as 'a' single community. Instead, the Report claimed that Britain is a 'community of communities' where our shared Britishness should be defined not by what makes a nation or region different, but what they have in common.[14]

---

[11] Ibid. He continued: 'Blood alone does not define our national identity. How can we separate out the Celtic, the Roman, the Saxon, the Norman, the Huguenot, the Jewish, – the Asian and the Caribbean and all the other nations that have come and settled here? Why should we want to? It is precisely this rich mix that has made all of us what we are today.'

[12] Ibid.

[13] See Runnymede Trust, 'Commission on the Future of Multi-Ethnic Britain'.

[14] See Bhikhu Parekh (ed), *The Future of Multi-Ethnic Britain: Report of the Commission on the Future of Multi-Ethnic Britain* (London: Profile, 2000): ix–x. See also Bhikhu Parekh, *Rethinking Multiculturalism: Cultural Diversity and Political Theory* (Basingstoke: Palgrave Macmillan, 2006): 201–202, 231–233.

However, in searching for this shared sense of belonging, the Parekh Report urged that we should not seek to base this sense on a fixed identity. The Parekh Report astutely recognizes that what it means to be British is not set in stone. It has changed over time and will continue to do so, shaped in different ways by its evolving past and future trajectories. The Report says that 'Britishness is an idea in transition' and we must continually question what this means for the here and now.[15] There is no one answer for eternity. While it was not an official government report, Parekh's recommendations have exerted a strong influence on the official reviews that followed.[16]

A second review group was led by Labour MP John Denham. The Denham Report published shortly after 9/11 claimed that 'it is ... essential to establish a greater sense of citizenship based on common principles that are shared by all sections of the community. The concept of citizenship would also place a higher value on cultural differences'.[17] It echoed ideas first found in the Parekh Report, agreeing that Britishness should be understood as a set of shared principles common to all who are British, emphasizing the need for inclusivity in light of the diversity of cultural and regional backgrounds.

The third review group – the 'Life in the UK' Advisory Group – was then created for the purposes of proposing how the government should launch new citizenship tests and citizenship ceremonies. The name comes from the British Nationality Act 1981 requirement that anyone applying to naturalize must possess 'sufficient knowledge about life in the United Kingdom', which the Nationality, Immigration

---

[15] Parekh, *The Future of Multi-Ethnic Britain*, xv.

[16] Parekh became a Labour Peer the year the report was published.

[17] See Home Office, *Building Cohesive Communities: A Report of the Ministerial Group on Public Order and Community Cohesion* (London: Home Office, 2001).

and Asylum Act 2002 made assessed by a 'life in the United Kingdom' citizenship test.[18] While the test's name pays literal homage to its legislative parentage, there is no reason why the test could not have been given a different name. Other countries name their tests and none, curiously, have picked a dry name dripping with legalese like '*Life in the ...*' for a title.

David Blunkett, now Lord Blunkett, plays a central role throughout from the legislation and Advisory Group's formation to its test launch. He had been Education Secretary prior to becoming Home Secretary in 2001, a background that Sara Wallace Goodman has claimed was important to his thinking, as Blunkett leaned heavily on educationalists on this Group, chaired by his former tutor when a student at the University of Sheffield, Professor Sir Bernard Crick.[19] At least eight of the 14 Advisory Group members were educationalists, including Crick. The citizenship test's original content was heavily influenced by what was part of the citizenship education programme of study offered at secondary schools.[20]

The Advisory Group was the first – and only – public consultation into what a test for British citizenship should be about. This work received widespread commentary, much of it cynical. BBC reporter Mark Easton remarked that defining Britishness was 'like painting wind'.[21] In *Watching the English*, Kate Fox observes that Britishness seems 'a rather meaningless

---

[18] See Schedule 1(1)(ca) of the British Nationality Act 1981 and s1 of the Nationality, Immigration and Asylum Act 2002.

[19] Sara Wallace Goodman, *Immigration and Membership Politics in Western Europe* (Cambridge: Cambridge University Press, 2014): 146.

[20] See Dina Kiwan, 'Active citizenship, multiculturalism and mutual understanding' in Bernard Crick and Andrew Lockyer (eds), *Active Citizenship: What Could It Achieve and How?* (Edinburgh: Edinburgh University Press, 2010): 100–111, at 107.

[21] Mark Easton, 'Define Britishness? It's like painting wind', BBC News (2 March 2012).

term'.[22] One interviewee I spoke to said trying to define Britishness "was like trying to grasp a will-o-the-wisp".

No doubt the initial responses to the Advisory Group are revealing. When asking about what is Britishness in different parts of the UK, the Group heard very different answers. In Scotland, the public would mention haggis (food always came up), Hogmanay and Scottish institutions like its legal system with its three verdicts of guilt, innocence and not proven. The Welsh claimed Welsh cakes, the Welsh language and flag were a part of being British. In southern England, Britishness meant the English language, England's patron saint and activities like Morris dancing. What was immediately apparent is local people were not pointing out what they had in common with other British citizens, but what made their locality different from the rest of the UK as it is from France. These differences – of Parekh's 'community of communities' – were what helped make the UK distinctive and a part of Britishness. The Group highlighted the need to address the 'lack of English or limited awareness of cultural differences' as well as increasing 'participative citizenship and community development'.[23]

Crick's Advisory Group followed the Parekh Report in claiming that the values of good British citizenship are the values of good citizenship anywhere.[24] The Group said that:

> To be British ... mean[s] that we respect the laws, the elected parliamentary and democratic political

[22] Kate Fox, *Watching the English: The Hidden Rules of English Behaviour* (London: Hodder, 2004).

[23] Home Office, *The New and the Old: The Report of the 'Life in the United Kingdom' Advisory Group* (London: Home Office Communication Directorate, 2003): paras 2.2–2.3.

[24] See Bridget Anderson, *Us and Them: The Dangerous Politics of Immigration Control* (Oxford: Oxford University Press, 2013): 107. See also Lee Jarvis, Lee Marsden and Eylem Atakav, 'Public conceptions and constructions of "British values": a qualitative analysis', *British Journal of Politics and International Relations* 22(1) (2020): 85–101.

structures, traditional values of mutual tolerance, respect for equal rights and mutual concerns, and that we give our allegiance to the state (as commonly symbolized in the Crown) in return for protection. To be British is to respect those over-arching specific institutions, values, beliefs and traditions that bind us all, the different nations and cultures together in peace and in a legal order.[25]

The Group's idea is that the creation of a baseline of values for a shared political identity can establish solidarity among different groups without sacrificing their differences.[26] We can be English or Welsh, Catholic or Muslim, rich or poor and accept these values – as can probably citizens of any other state. The UK citizenship test should focus on these shared values and the range of important cultural, social and political distinctive characteristics across all four nations.[27]

The view espoused by the Crick Report is summed up well by former Prime Minister Gordon Brown, who said:

The values and qualities I describe are of course to be found in many other cultures and countries. But when taken together, and as they shape the institutions of our country, these values and qualities – being creative, adaptable and outward looking, our belief in liberty, duty and fair play – add up to a distinctive Britishness that has been manifest throughout our history, and shaped it.[28]

---

[25] Home Office, *The New and the Old*, 8.

[26] See Goodman, *Immigration and Membership Politics in Western Europe*, 35.

[27] Later Crick remarked that Britishness 'refers to a narrow if strong and important political and legal culture: the Union itself, the rule of law, the Crown and Parliament, perhaps the practice of a common political citizenship'. See Bernard Crick, 'Identity politics' in Bernard Crick and Andrew Lockyer (eds), *Active Citizenship: What Could It Achieve and How?* (Edinburgh: Edinburgh University Press, 2010): 193.

[28] Quoted in ibid, 194.

In practical terms, the Group recommended a flexible programme of studies covering six broad categories: 'British national institutions in recent historical context', 'Britain as a multicultural society', 'knowing the law', 'employment', 'sources of help and information' and 'everyday needs'.[29] It recommended that prospective citizens learn together as a group, enabling peer support, and that the test handbook should be available free of charge.[30]

As will be seen, not all recommendations were accepted. Chapters on British history and law were included in the test handbook, but explicitly not included as a part of any test. This was in the face of criticism that the historical chapter contained contested claims. The government rejected the idea that most applicants should be encouraged to learn citizenship together in favour of a more individualistic approach, putting the onus on applicants to seek out information and pass. Nor has the test handbook been free, unlike other test texts such as in Australia and the United States.

But this leaves a fundamental question: is this a test about whether someone *is 'British'* or has a sufficiently strong knowledge *about 'Britain'*? This is a crucial distinction. In other words, does passing the test help confirm the achievement of a new identity or a kind of qualification based on memorization? At the time of its 2005 launch, there remained a deep confusion.

This is brought out well by then Immigration Minister Tony McNulty who said: 'This is not a test of someone's ability to be British or a test of their Britishness. It is a test of their preparedness to become citizens.'[31] Because it was about looking forward, the government did not think it was crucial for British history to be covered on the test.[32] This

---

[29] Home Office, *The Old and the New*, paras 3.2–3.8.

[30] Ibid, para. 4.2.

[31] C. Taylor, *ESOL and Citizenship: A Teacher's Guide* (Leicester: NIACE, 2007).

[32] See BBC News, 'New UK citizenship testing starts' (1 November 2005).

raises further questions about how the test can be expected to examine knowledge of traditions without considering their history or context.[33] Moreover, it is unclear what precisely it means to be tested on preparedness for becoming British, but not 'being' British. After all, a British citizen is, well, British.

If McNulty is right, why claim the best – or only – way to 'test' being ready for citizenship is literally through a civic knowledge test? For example, as remarked to me in conversation by Bhikhu Parekh some years ago, we can test whether someone has sufficient knowledge of life in the UK by whether they have made a life here, resided here for a period of time (such as five years) and whether they have made positive contributions as a law-abiding, tax-paying resident and so on. To live such a life demands knowledge of how to engage successfully in this country and can be evidenced through performance. And this might appear to capture better what really matters, namely, whether someone can live successfully in the UK in accordance with its cherished public values and make a contribution to the community rather than as a pointless bureaucratic exercise to confirm if somebody merely ticks the right boxes when asked on a multiple-choice exam. Claiming to hold values is different from being able to evidence a respect for them. So why not test knowledge of life in the UK like this – looking at residency, good character and the like – rather than this test? This would prioritize performance over a memory check.

Parekh's insightful remarks are echoed by the influential Canadian political theorist Joseph Carens, who says:

> Tests of civic competence never actually test civic competence. The tests that assess a person's knowledge of various facts about the history and institutions of

---

[33] Ibid.

the country tell us nothing about a person's civic capacities. Citizens have to make political judgements. The knowledge required for wise political judgement is complex, multifaceted and often intuitive. It's not something that can be captured on a test.[34]

For Carens, citizenship tests are problematic when expected to do too much. No test can confirm civic competence, at least not by itself. Provided their scope is limited and not intended primarily as a means to exclude, Carens believes tests can be justified on a limited basis only.[35] As we shall see, the 'Life in the UK' test lacks such a basis, undermining its normative justification.

In contrast, the leading political philosopher David Miller is more supportive of tests than Carens. He claims that they are justifiable where providing useful knowledge with normative guidance, such as the value and limits of free speech.[36] This is important as these conditions are not satisfied by the 'Life in the UK' citizenship test. Miller agrees with Carens that the test might not compel an immigrant to *adopt* specific values. However, it has importance, for Miller, in that it does force some *recognition* of them as they must be recalled to pass the test.[37] Of course, one learns about life in the UK by living, not by standardized tests, as Devyani Prabhat has

---

[34] Joseph H. Carens, *The Ethics of Immigration* (Oxford: Oxford University Press, 2013): 59.

[35] In defence of Carens, Gillian Brock claims 'tests that are designed to exclude because they are too difficult are clearly unjust'. While I agree with this view, I do not take it as obvious or assumed as it appears to be by Brock. I will spell out later that a main problem is that, if we wished to find a means to exclude, there are other more efficient and transparent ways of doing it – which renders using a citizenship test to that end as unjustified. (See Brock, *Migration and Political Theory*, 84.)

[36] David Miller, *Strangers in Our Midst: The Political Philosophy of Immigration* (Cambridge, MA: Harvard University Press, 2016): 137.

[37] See ibid, 138.

pointed out correctly.[38] But such a test, for Miller, if well designed, can help us reflect more about the life we have as prospective citizens. Citizenship tests can play a useful role even if, again, they are not expected to do too much and do not by themselves confer civic competence. So, while the key academics working in this area adopt different conclusions, there is some support for a test if used in this limited and specific way.

Another relevant issue is what passing a test is supposed to achieve. Today, the citizenship test is now a requirement for becoming a British citizen. Contrary to what McNulty said at the test's launch, perhaps the test is not a test of being British but those who pass are well on their way to becoming British in terms of citizenship. This raises a question about whether this is really about a legal or political 'Britishness' versus something more cultural or social. As one of my Durham University colleagues once remarked to me, "even though you might have lived in Britain longer than they've been alive, many of your students will always see you as American not British – how strange that is". Of course, many do not see this – or me – in this way.

But the point is the idea of a *citizenship test* in the form of a standardized exam can be no more than one part of a wider assessment for conferring the legal and political rights of British citizenship. The UK is not unique and is part of a global wave of countries using citizenship tests to help meet the requirements for settlement and naturalization.[39] And yet, as we shall see, many of the tests have become ever more complex and technical, creating barriers instead of bridges built on unrealistic assumptions about what citizens do know, what they should know and the ability of a multiple-choice

---

[38] See Devyani Prabhat, *Britishness, Belonging and Citizenship: Experiencing Nationality Law* (Bristol: Policy Press, 2018): 105.

[39] See Tamar de Waal, *Integration Requirements for Immigrants in Europe: A Legal-Philosophical Inquiry* (Oxford: Hart, 2021).

exam to confirm a readiness for good citizenship. Worse still, the consultation used to establish the UK's use of the test has never been followed up to see if the aims and purposes were achieved, or how they might be improved.

THREE

A New Beginning

The new test launched in November 2005 and was considered by most commentators to be a resounding flop. While the government had taken its time to conduct a national conversation about what the test should include via the Advisory Group, it gave very little time for the Group to design the test and its handbook.

Notably, there were errors galore. The original edition got wrong where Charles II lived in exile, claiming he was in France when, in fact, he was in Holland.[1] Then the test handbook required memorizing a misquote from Sir Winston Churchill. Applicants had to say his words were that 'never in the course of human conflict have so many owed so much to so few'.[2] Instead, Churchill had actually said 'never in the field of human conflict was so much owed by so many to so few'.[3] Not all mistakes were historical. For example, the test handbook wrongly claims Northern Ireland is a part of Great Britain, which is composed instead of England, Scotland and Wales.[4]

While most of the original test handbook's headline-grabbing errors are found in its first chapter on British history, this probably had a greater negative bearing on public confidence about the test than pass rates. This is partly because the history

---

[1] See Home Office, *Life in the United Kingdom: A Journey to Citizenship* (London: The Stationery Office, 2005): 28 (hereafter '*First Edition*').

[2] Ibid, 37.

[3] See Home Office, *Third Edition*, 57.

[4] See Home Office, *First Edition*, 17.

chapter in the test handbook was explicitly noted as being included for information-only purposes: none of its content was covered in any test. The test's textual errors may have all been accidental, but they were also largely foreseeable given the circumstances of its creation and launch.

The first test was a rushed, botched job. It states upfront that the Advisory Group 'tried hard to check all the facts cited, and we apologise if there are mistakes or important omissions'.[5] This is an astonishing admission as the facts as presented make a substantive difference both to whether someone passes the test and may become a British citizen and to whether the test does help ensure integration of migrants. The clear implication is that the test's correct answers might not all be true and this admission can give an appearance of not taking its aim and purpose seriously, as if it did then greater care might be taken to avoid errors and mistaken omissions.

The history chapter singled out for its factual errors was single-authored by Sir Bernard Crick.[6] Most of the other chapters were more of a group effort and the test handbook is subtitled 'published on behalf of the Life in the United Kingdom Advisory Group' – even though this had morphed, since 19 November 2004, into the Advisory Board on Naturalisation and Integration, who were supported by 'University for Industry' (UfI).[7] When asked by the *Guardian* about why there were so many problems with getting the facts right, Crick was refreshingly candid, admitting that 'there are errors in it because it was done fairly quickly because we didn't want to keep immigrants waiting for their citizenship'.[8] At issue was that citizenship grants were being held up until

---

[5] Ibid, 9 note 1.

[6] Ibid, 9.

[7] See Baroness Scotland of Asthal, 'Citizenship', House of Lords debate, 22 November 2005, column 200; learndirect, 'Company history'.

[8] Lee Glendinning, 'Citizenship guide fails its history exam', *The Guardian* (29 April 2006).

applicants had passed the test, requiring some to wait until a test was launched. This rushed effort is further noticeable in the poor presentation of the text, including typographical errors even on its cover.[9]

The most glaring problem, for me, is that the test handbook got wrong the number of Members of Parliament. The test handbook claims that there were 645 when there was one more.[10] To my surprise, this error was not picked up by any commentator until my 2013 report.[11] It might be thought obvious that if the government got any facts right it would have been how many MPs sit in Parliament, yet this has been an issue since the test's launch.

My best attempt at explaining this mistake about MPs is that the candidate for Staffordshire South, the Liberal Democrat Josephine Harrison, had died on 30 April 2005. This was a few days before a General Election held on 5 May. A special election was held in June where the seat was retained for the Conservatives by Sir Patrick Cormack, now Baron Cormack, which meant 645 MPs were sworn in together. I can only assume that this news of 645 MPs forming a new Parliament post-election is where this figure for the test handbook has come from. The 646th member was sworn in later after the special election and so overlooked by the test. It should be shocking that no one in Parliament noticed the error.

---

[9] The cover notes 'For Life in the UK Test visit www.lifeintheuktest.gov. uk' and not 'For the Life in the UK test'. See also Home Office, *First Edition*, 51.

[10] Ibid, 61.

[11] Brooks, *The 'Life in the United Kingdom' Citizenship Test*, 11. The Home Office was likely aware as it corrected this number to 646 for the second edition, but left this unchanged when the number of MPs was increased to 650. See Home Office, *Life in the United Kingdom: A Journey to Citizenship, 2nd edition* (London: The Stationery Office, 2007): 44 (hereafter '*Second Edition*').

Perhaps just as damaging for the test's reputation was not merely what it got wrong, but what it thought was right to include. An example singled out for widespread ridicule was about what to do if you accidentally spill someone's drink in a pub. The answer is to apologise and offer to buy another.[12] Illustrations like this led the *London Review of Books* to claim the UK citizenship test handbook was 'the funniest book currently available in the English language'.[13] A theme of the various criticisms was that such everydayness was best 'tested' through experience, like visiting a pub, and not taking a multiple-choice exam.

It became clear almost from the test's launch that it would need to be substantially corrected and revised. But how? Jill Rutter has noted a deep division at the heart of the test's purpose. Those seeing the main aim as economic integration wanted content focused on the knowledge and skills needed to acquire work. Others advocating for cultural integration wanted content emphasizing culture and values. This lack of conceptual clarity – is the test to facilitate economic or cultural integration? – adds an unnecessary confusion right at the heart of the test.[14] The problem is further evident in explicitly not testing the error-ridden chapter on British history ('The making of the United Kingdom') while acknowledging in the test handbook's introduction that:

> some history is *essential* for understanding the culture of any new country, and can help in following references in ordinary conversation by British people who themselves may not think they know much history but whose sense of national history nonetheless echoes past events

---

[12] Home Office, *First Edition*, 101.

[13] Andrew O'Hagan, 'A journey to citizenship', *London Review of Books* 28(23) (30 November 2006).

[14] See Jill Rutter, *Moving Up and Getting On: Migration, Integration and Social Cohesion in the UK* (Bristol: Policy Press, 2015): 69.

and beliefs. We British are very fond, for instance, of 'the Dunkirk spirit', 'the Nelson touch' or 'she's a real Florence Nightingale'.[15]

It begs the question of why omit 'essential' information for integrating into an inclusive British culture on a test aimed at ensuring integration? This is a crucial mistake given the test's aim of supporting integration.[16] As former Home Secretary Jacqui Smith remarked to me, "the principle is right" about the citizenship test.[17] The issue is getting right which multiple-choice questions and answers realize its aims and purposes. This challenge shows no sign of going away, as we shall see with future test editions.

In conclusion, the UK government moved too swiftly to implement and launch a citizenship test on the back of three successive and successful reports led by Parekh, Denham and Crick. This rush led to errors of fact and omissions as well as a lack of conceptual clarity about its central purpose. Caught in the middle were migrants applying for citizenship who became forced to learn facts, some of which were untrue, and without the peer support recommended by the Advisory Group in having citizenship classes.

Instead, the test of being a part of the community as a prospective citizen with others was a road travelled alone by individuals where integration was a one-way street. While the test was launched with the hope of making naturalization more meaningful and ensure new citizens had 'a sense of belonging to a wider community',[18] the test had few public supporters, attracted stinging criticisms and an effort was made almost

---

[15] Home Office, *First Edition*, 13 (emphasis added).
[16] For example, see comments of Life in the UK Advisory Group member Dina Kiwan in 'A journey to citizenship in the United Kingdom', *International Journal on Multicultural Societies* 10(1) (2008): 60–75.
[17] 'Interview with Jacqui Smith', 28 September 2015.
[18] David Blunkett quoted in Home Office, *First Edition*, 11.

immediately to correct its errors – but without consulting anyone who sat it and without any review of whether its intended purposes were being met. The test became just another tick box exercise the public had little confidence in. This inability to consult or review is a persistent failure that has only made problems worse over time. These problems matter as they can make the difference between who is or is not a British citizen.[19]

---

[19] This includes non-British members of the Royal Family, such as the Duchess of Sussex. If she wanted to become a British citizen, she would have to pass to the citizenship test. There are exemptions, but not on account of her being a member of that family. See Thom Brooks, 'Good luck with the citizenship test, Meghan Markle. It's a mess', *The Guardian* (1 March 2018). See Thom Brooks, *The Trust Factor: Essays on the Current Political Crisis and Hope for the Future* (London: Methuen, 2022).

FOUR

Not Learning from Mistakes

Less than two years after the first edition was published, a new second edition of the test handbook appeared in 2007.[1] The test's design was led once again by the Advisory Board on Naturalisation and Integration, but with a new chair, Mary Coussey, following Sir Bernard Crick's retirement in May 2005. The Home Secretary's Foreword to the second edition, by John Reid, now Lord Reid of Cardowan, thanks 'heartily' the Board's members for their having 'led this task' of revising 'this handbook thoroughly'.[2] This echoes the explicit claims in the first edition that it was a product of this independent group, which has the further benefit of insulating the government from direct criticisms arising from any defects with the test.

However, an official memorandum from July 2008 concerning the closure of this Board notes that it offered only 'ad hoc advice' about the test and 'other integration issues'.[3] In Parliament a month earlier, Home Office minister Liam Byrne said the questions were 'drawn up by experts

---

[1] See Home Office, *Second Edition*, 28.

[2] Ibid, iii.

[3] See Matthew Coats, 'Letter' (11 July 2008). Coats was a civil servant with the position of Head of Immigration. The letter notes Advisory Board members have included Celine Castelino, Mary Curnock Cook, Sally Daghlian, Sir Robert Dowling, Samina Khan, Jan Luff, Adeeba Malik, Elizabeth Meehan, David Muir, Sir Gulam Noon, Ashok Ohri, Julia Onslow-Cle, Maeve Sherlock, Jean Wilson, Patrick Wintour and Annette Zera alongside Crick and Coussey.

in computer-based assessment from UfI (the organisation that holds the current contract for providing the testing service) and representatives from the Advisory Board for Naturalisation and Integration. The current database of test questions was approved by Ministers'.[4] In other words, on the one hand, the government was claiming publicly the main work for the test was done by an independent Board while, on the other hand, it said privately that its contribution was only 'ad hoc', giving the appearance of creating a scapegoat to protect the government from any further problems with the new test. However, while Crick was singled out for criticism over the first edition where he played a clear leading role, the government was unable to pin the blame on others for its new edition as the name on the front was the Home Secretary's and the Board was disbanded shortly after the new test was launched.

The second edition saw itself as an updated and expanded version of the original test handbook, or what it should have looked like if there was sufficient time to put it together. A few chapter titles were amended, such as chapter 3 (from 'Britain Today: A Profile' to 'UK Today: A Profile') and chapter 4 (from 'How Britain is Governed' to 'How the United Kingdom is Governed'). Much of the text corrects, revises or expands on the first edition. The first edition's first chapter on history begins: 'To understand a country well and the character of its inhabitants, some history is needed.'[5] The second edition renders this more readable: 'To understand a country it is important to know something about its history.'[6] Despite claiming knowledge about British history is 'needed' (first edition) and 'important' (second edition), neither edition includes any questions about this topic. There is also a new

---

[4] Liam Byrne MP, 'British nationality: assessments', House of Commons debate, 18 June 2008, column 961.

[5] Home Office, *First Edition*, 17.

[6] Home Office, *Second Edition*, 7.

chapter ('Building Better Communities') and a new glossary containing over 400 terms. There is no clear philosophical shift in how British citizenship was conceived and Tony Blair was Prime Minister when both editions were published.[7]

One overlooked change is the reduction of telephone numbers and websites listed in the test handbook that were not explicitly ruled out as possible information that applicants might have to memorize to pass the test. The first edition includes 31 telephone numbers and 49 websites, such as the number for the National Academic Recognition Information Centre (NARIC) for the UK noting 01242 260010 and fax number 01242 258611 as well as the website for the People's Dispensary for Sick Animals which is www.pdsa.org.uk.[8] These telephone numbers and website addresses could generate 80 unique test questions for more than three unique tests.

The second edition includes 36 telephone numbers and 23 websites. These include how to contact Members of Parliament or the regional governments in Wales, Scotland and Northern Ireland as well as the emergency services. There are others like the Association of British Credit Unions' website at www.abcul.coop and the telephone number for Energywatch at 0845 906 0708.[9] The second edition retains the first edition's inclusion of NARIC's telephone number.[10] The second edition contains enough numbers and website for 59 unique questions for more than two unique tests.

---

[7]   It is worth noting that Tony Blair was Prime Minister when the first and second editions were published. Gordon Brown became Prime Minister in June 2007 a few months after the second edition appeared in April 2007. Events since the first test was launched in November 2004, such as 7/7, did not appear to contribute to any changes in the test either. If anything, according to conversations that I have had with those involved at the time, such events further reinforced the need for the citizenship test rather than a change to it.

[8]   Home Office, *First Edition*, 102, 109.

[9]   Home Office, *Second Edition*, 58, 61.

[10]   Ibid, 76.

While this reduction in the total number of telephone numbers and websites might look like progress – after all, who thinks memorizing such information should be *required* for becoming British? – it is somewhat elusory. The second edition came with an *Official Citizenship Study Guide*, providing over 200 practice test questions across all test areas.[11] While the official guide claims its wording is not the exact same as found on the actual tests, it aims to offer an official and clear expectation about the kinds of questions, question formats and answers that are on the tests. It is noteworthy that none ask about any telephone numbers or websites notwithstanding the test handbook claims all its information – save for two chapters – could be on a test. It would appear this claim is untrue, as not all information found in testable chapters is actually used on any test.

One innovation with the second edition was the publication of an aforementioned companion *Official Citizenship Test Study Guide*.[12] This was helpful in highlighting for applicants what test questions, formats and answers look like to help prepare for the actual test. Curiously, the *Study Guide* is explicit that its *practice* questions 'are *not* the actual questions … in the test'.[13] Instead, they are meant to represent what kinds of questions can be expected, not what exact questions an applicant might find.

This was not my experience at all. When I sat the second edition in 2009, I recall seeing questions verbatim on the test as listed in the *Study Guide*, raising questions about its real purposes: why not share actual questions if this information is thought essential and beneficial for becoming a citizen? And is the purpose of practice questions not actually found on any test to deter would-be applicants, irrespective of the merits of

---

[11] Home Office, *Official Citizenship Test Study Guide* (London: The Stationery Office, 2007) (hereafter '*Second Edition: Study Guide*').

[12] Ibid.

[13] Ibid, v (emphasis original).

their case for citizenship? In other words, why make the test a tougher barrier – one that most citizens cannot actually pass themselves? This barrier causes problems, as will become clear.

Test questions came in three different varieties: the good, the bad and the downright ugly. The 'good' questions are ones that the public might expect and be familiar with. These include questions like whether 'the Geordie dialect is spoken in Tyneside' (which is true – and I took the test myself in Newcastle upon Tyne) or knowing that the HMRC is the 'government department … responsible for collecting taxes'.[14] Another example is knowing that fireworks are traditionally set off on 5 November.[15]

There are also badly formulated 'good' questions. My favourite example is the play on words options for what does GCSE stand for. The correct answer is 'General Certificate of Secondary Education', but the tricky false options include 'Graduate Certificate of Secondary Education' or 'Grade Certificate of School Education'.[16] Unfortunately, the test is not exclusively a test of good questions badly formulated or not.

But there are other kinds of 'bad' questions. This is where the correct answer when the test goes to print remains the correct answer even though it is no longer true, such as when departments or statistics became outdated and change. Some examples include knowing the population of the UK, but only in 2001 where the general population of 60 million was very different than estimated by 2013 at over 64 million.[17] When I sat the test, the UK's population was just over 62 million.[18] While the test listed 62 million as a possible answer and the

---

[14] Ibid, 38, 84.

[15] Ibid, 42. The occasion is Guy Fawkes Night, which is noted in the second edition test handbook. (Home Office, *Second Edition*, 41.)

[16] See Home Office, *Second Edition: Study Guide*, 29.

[17] Ibid, 38.

[18] See Office for National Statistics, *Overview of the UK Population: January 2021* (14 January 2021).

actual population, the correct answer for the test was two million less because it used the earlier census data for the right answer. So, applicants needed to know the size of the UK's population from years earlier and answering with the current figure would count as incorrect. Another illustration is the test's correct answer for the proportion of young people in higher education in the UK (1 in 3, when as of writing it is 1 in 2).[19]

A key example of a bad question is the persistent problem the test has had with the number of MPs.[20] As noted in the last chapter, the first test edition mistakenly claimed there were 645 MPs in Parliament when there were actually 646. The second edition corrected this, but then Parliament changed the number of constituencies in 2010 to 650.[21] This change was not made to the test, meaning that the test still required prospective citizens to state the wrong number of MPs to get this question right – and all as evidence of demonstrating knowledge of life in the UK sufficient to meet the legal requirement. A similar problem was also found with the then number of Members of the European Parliament listed as 78, but the actual number was later changed to 72 prior to the UK leaving the European Union.[22] The situation is farcical.

And then there are the downright 'ugly' questions which make a mockery of the exercise. Take the question of where can you find details of trade unions in the UK? The correct answer is the Trades Union Congress (TUC) website, but is it always true that the alternative answer, 'local library', would not also be able to provide such information?[23] Unlikely. Another

---

[19] See Home Office, *Second Edition: Study Guide*, 26 and Sean Coughlan, 'The symbolic target of 50% at university reached', BBC News (26 September 2019).

[20] See Home Office, *Second Edition: Study Guide*, 54.

[21] See Neil Johnston, *Constituency Boundary Reviews and the Number of MPs*, House of Commons Library (London: Parliament, 8 June 2021).

[22] See Home Office, *Second Edition: Study Guide*, 56.

[23] Ibid, 85.

is the question of from which two places can you get advice if you are having trouble at work and need to take further action? The correct answers are Citizens' Advice Bureau and the national Advisory, Conciliation and Arbitration Service (ACAS). But the two wrong answers – your local MP and your employer – aren't wrong as places you could not ever get such advice.[24] What's missing is qualifying the test question with 'from which two *independent* places can you gain advice?' No doubt speaking with one's employer about work problems is often an essential first step in most cases.

A second ugly question is asking where young people from families with low income can get financial help with their studies when they leave school at age 16. The correct answer was 'Education Maintenance Allowance'.[25] The only problem is that this was scrapped, but left unchanged on the test. So, applicants had to know about a scheme they could never access because it no longer existed. But knowing they might access the defunct scheme if it did still exist was thought enough, in part, to demonstrate suitability for British citizenship.

My favourite example of an ugly question is from the second edition – and it was on my test taken in 2009. The question asks 'which two places can you go to if you need a National Insurance number?'[26] Of course, most non-naturalized British citizens simply receive this in the post. But on the test, applicants were required to correctly guess the *two* places you could go and the answer is only counted as correct if both correct answers are given. The options listed were the Department for Education and Skills, the Home Office, Jobcentre Plus and the Social Security Office. The last two options are the 'correct' answers, but there is a twist.[27] While this question was being asked, the Social Security Office ceased to exist.

---

[24] Ibid, 86.

[25] Ibid, 72.

[26] Ibid, 14.

[27] See Home Office, *Second Edition*, 80.

Applicants for British citizenship proving their knowledge of life in the UK were required to claim on a Home Office-approved test that they could get their National Insurance number from a government office that no longer existed and so this could not, in fact, happen. Similarly, there was no longer a Department for Education and Skills as this had been reorganized. All the more baffling for me was that I had received my National Insurance number from neither of the correct answers, but after an interview at the Department for Work and Pensions – where I was directed after phoning the Home Office. While I did know how to get my number and did it, I had to claim two different ways were the only options even though one did not then exist either.

Whether good, bad or ugly, the second edition contained errors that only multiplied over time. The official answer to whether a judge decides who is guilty or innocent of an innocent crime is 'false', as this is done by a jury.[28] But, in fact, it is possible to have a serious crime heard in the Crown Court without a jury where the judge determines guilt or innocence.[29] I have already flagged answers that were either incorrect at the time the test was released or soon afterwards regarding the number of MPs, who can claim a non-existent Education Maintenance Allowance and where to get a National Insurance number to name a few. These problems were fuelled by a heavy reliance on the 2001 census that was updated a decade later in 2011.[30] Thus, large parts of some chapters required memorizing demographic information that was out of date and an inaccurate picture of the Britain that successful test applicants hoped to join as citizens.

To be clear, this was denied by the government when challenged in 2012. The then Immigration Minister Damian

---

[28] See Home Office, *Second Edition: Study Guide*, 52.

[29] For example, see Crown Prosecution Service, 'Non-jury trials'.

[30] See Office for National Statistics, *2011 Census*.

Green claimed 'all questions asked *in the current test* are factually correct. Questions are based on the Life in the UK handbook, which includes information from the 2001 census. Any questions based on information which is no longer accurate are removed from the question bank'.[31]

Responding a few months later to a written question from Labour MP Chi Onwurah, Green said: 'We are aware that the existing handbook has some out-of-date information, which will be remedied by the publication of a new edition. In the meantime, questions for the life in the UK test which are no longer valid are in any case removed from the question bank.'[32] When I took the test prior to this statement in June 2012, this was not the case and other interviewees I have spoken with report similarly finding outdated or inaccurate questions on their tests. Given the new attention to the test's problems from 2011, it would be unsurprising if action was taken then, if not earlier, to ensure the test was accurate. Either way, there seems to have been no attention to, or discussion about, problems with the test's content in the second edition until after I called them out.

The second edition has been described as 'even *more* about life in the United Kingdom than its predecessor had been' with its additional information about government programmes and practicalities.[33] Maybe so, but while the

---

[31] Damian Green MP, 'British nationality: assessments', House of Commons debate, 25 June 2012, column 29. Emphasis added.

[32] See Chi Onwurah MP and Damian Green MP, 'British nationality: assessments', House of Commons debate, 5 September 2012, column 350. Chi was the first Member of Parliament I spoke with about problems with the citizenship test after appearing on a panel together about immigration at the Tyneside Irish Centre in Newcastle upon Tyne. If not for her support and encouragement, I might not have persevered these many years since in pressing for a citizenship test that is fit for purpose.

[33] See Kerry Ryan, 'Citizenship by the booklet', *Inside Story* (5 March 2013) (emphasis added).

second edition of the test corrected actual inaccuracies in the first edition, it embedded a new design flaw. The second edition placed heavier emphasis on knowing about different government departments and programmes – at a time when the New Labour government in power was at the zenith of its reforming and reorganizing zeal. So, many of the departments and programmes to be known for the test published in 2007 soon became frequently changed, merged with others or terminated. Meanwhile, the test was not updated until a new edition in 2013. This led to an increasing number of 'correct' answers on the test that were factually untrue, as I will reveal shortly.

My research has shown that it became possible within a few years of the second edition's launch to have a test of 24 questions where *all* correct answers were *factually untrue*.[34] And, no one in government, opposition benches or the mainstream media was aware. Meanwhile, the Magna Carta, Britain's role in two world wars and the right to silence and free speech were all information that no one seeking British citizenship was required to know. This was because the chapters on British history and basic law are in the test handbook, but not included on any test.

These serious problems gained added significance under this second edition. This is because – starting with the second edition and continuing to this day – the UK's 'citizenship' took on the dual purpose of being a test for permanent residency as well. This is not reflected in the second edition's subtitle ('A Journey to Citizenship'), but is in the third edition ('A Guide for New Residents'). So, not only was everyone applying for naturalization required to pass a flawed test with wrong 'correct' answers, but also everyone wanting Indefinite Leave to Remain. Tens of thousands more

---

[34] See Thom Brooks, 'The British citizenship test: the case for reform', *Political Quarterly* 83(3) (2012): 560–566.

people were now taking a test to remain or become citizens that was error-prone, contained trick questions and no one noticed the mistakes until I called it out after they had already become widespread.[35]

That the test had become a smorgasbord of trivia about UK programmes and institutions – many of which non-EU citizens applying for permanent residency could not access anyway. Understandably, the test was perceived by almost every one of the more than 200 people that I have interviewed about the test as an exercise in regurgitating mostly useless or unimportant facts that most British citizens do not know or are require to understand. An ineffective way of testing integration where only the applicants are required to know facts that citizens do not.

Because only applicants for permanent residency or citizenship can take – and so see – the actual test, it is unsurprising to find the public generally unaware of its existence and contents. This extends to much academic comment, too. For example, the political philosopher David Miller claims 'the content of the tests themselves are generally not demanding, requiring mainly learning the approved answers to a series of questions'.[36] So, while tests *could* be overly demanding and a barrier, this is not how we might expect them to be.

As already noted, the 'Life in the UK' test fails to meet these expectations as its approved answers can often be factually untrue and questions about the function of departments that no longer exist or of programmes discontinued seem clearly overly demanding, even reckless. And all the while successive governments claimed that immigration was a top issue that they took seriously, without noticing problems like this on the front-line that any immigrant in the system knew well. Until my BBC Radio 4 interview in 2011 and subsequent

---

[35] See BBC Radio 4, 'You and yours' (10 October 2011) (from 23 minutes).
[36] Miller, *Strangers in Our Midst*, 137.

campaigning for change, there were virtually no criticisms of the second edition's content.[37]

To be fair, Miller makes an exception for the UK, claiming 'it is doubtful if many UK-born citizens could achieve the 75 percent grade without preparing specifically for the test'.[38] If specified knowledge is held to be essential or otherwise important for someone to become a British citizen, it should be information that those already British citizens might be expected to know. It should be shocking that this is untrue, and perhaps even more alarming that it is so widely accepted to be untrue even by government ministers. In a memorable debate in the House of Lords held in 2013, the government minister, Lord Taylor of Holbeach, was asked if he had passed the test and he replied 'I have a sample test here and it is very fortunate that the correct answers are given in bold type'.[39] His Conservative Peer colleague Baroness Gardner of Parkes notes in the same debate that 'I have been in this country for almost 60 years. I could not possibly pass that test'.[40] If government ministers are unable to pass the test, why expect anyone else to?

Perhaps nothing better exemplifies this issue than what happened to then Prime Minister David Cameron on US television. While on a visit to America, Cameron was asked to appear on *The Late Show with David Letterman*, a late night talk show. Letterman surprised Cameron by asking him questions relating to the UK's second-edition citizenship test – which Cameron flunked.[41] If the Prime Minister could not answer

---

[37] See Damian Green MP, 'Clause 39', House of Commons debate, 11 June 2009, column 78 (complaining that citizenship test should not be able to be sat as many times as necessary until it is passed).

[38] Miller, *Strangers in Our Midst*, 138.

[39] Lord Taylor of Holbeach, 'Citizenship test – question', House of Lords debate, 26 February 2013, column 954.

[40] Baroness Gardner of Parkes, 'Citizenship test – question', House of Lords debate, 26 February 2013, column 955.

[41] See Nicholas Watt, 'David Cameron flunks citizenship test on David Letterman's Late Show', *The Guardian* (27 September 2012).

correctly most questions, it should be shocking that migrants are expected to get it right – all so they can show they have the same 'knowledge of life in the United Kingdom' as citizens who don't know the answers either.

It is regularly pointed out that the 'Life in the UK' citizenship test has a relatively high pass rate.[42] Over 70 per cent pass the test each year. Citizens of Australia and America, fellow Anglophone countries with strong historical links to the UK and with citizenship tests of their own, generally do best at over 95 per cent success. Citizens from other countries, especially from non-Anglophone areas and non-Commonwealth countries fare much less well.[43] This has remained constant since.[44] A high pass rate is not evidence that the test is unproblematic. Applicants must pass in order to remain in the UK or become citizens. It should be expected that those taking the test will make some attempt to become familiar with its contents given the importance of passing. But a test with so many false 'correct' answers and outdated material should never be a basis for trying to test integration. No matter how high the score, this is more evidence of a barrier overcome not a bridge crossed to becoming British.

In conclusion, the second edition was less rushed but no less problematic than the first edition. A key problem was its expanded coverage of demographics, public institutions and government programmes that often became outdated with

---

[42] Lord Taylor of Holbeach, 'Citizenship test – question', column 955. Lord Taylor suggests that a high pass rate on the Home Office's sample test – with questions not actually on the real test – is evidence that the real test is reasonable and fit for purpose. He notes in the same debate that he's only seen a practice test and does not claim to have ever seen the actual test questions.

[43] See BBC News, 'British citizenship test: one in three immigrants fails' (27 May 2010).

[44] See Holly Lynch MP and Kevin Foster MP, 'British nationality: assessments', Question for the Home Office, UIN 144730, tabled 27 January 2021.

population changes, Whitehall reorganizations and programme alternations leading up to a new test published in 2013, about six years after the second edition. The test was not amended or revised to account for any changes. And as more people sat the test, none were ever called on for feedback nor was there any official study to see whether the first tests met their original aims and purposes. These policy failings continued.

FIVE

From Trivia to Trivial

Despite widespread criticisms of the first edition accompanying its launch, there seemed little media or political interest in the citizenship test. While hundreds of thousands have taken the test for permanent residency or citizenship, there was virtually no coverage other than the occasional quiz in local papers for readers to see if they could pass such a test and few mentions in Parliament that correct answers on the citizenship test were sometimes factually wrong.[1] Yet, it was clear to anyone familiar with the test that it was increasingly unfit for purpose and required urgent reforms.

It can only be speculated that the reason these problems went unnoticed for so long was because few, if any, took seriously the voices of immigrants in the immigration system. Media coverage and political discourse was a conversation reserved for British citizens alone, with little interest in the experiences of immigrants. There was no effort at consulting with either citizens old or new nor with prospective applicants to become clearer on expectations and learn more about how well the test met its original aims and purposes. It was simply taken for granted – by political leaders from across the political spectrum who had not naturalized themselves – that passing this test

---

[1]   For some of the few examples pre-2011, see Nick Clegg MP, 'Naturalisation test', House of Commons debate, 16 April 2007, column 470 and 'Naturalisation test', House of Commons debate, 20 April 2007, column 830.

was somehow evidence that an immigrant had sufficiently integrated. There was no need to ask those who had done it or researched whether these assumptions were valid. Immigrant voices carried little, if any, weight.

This situation was vivid for me as I heard constant calls for immigration reforms from policy-makers and their supporters who had no experience of immigration or naturalizing themselves. Shortly after I obtained my British citizenship in 2011, I resolved to change that and lobby for citizenship test reform.[2] Through a local connection at BBC Newcastle, I was interviewed on BBC Radio 4's 'You and Yours' programme.[3] Originally, their plan was to interview then Home Secretary Theresa May alongside me, but she declined.[4] My interview was recorded on a Thursday. I claimed there was an urgent need for a new, third edition of the test. It needed to revise and refresh. Outdated and incorrect material needed correction. But I also took aim at the test's contents, arguing that the test should cover essential elements of British history and culture.

The programme aired the following Monday. That same day, after being alerted to my comments beforehand, the then Prime Minister David Cameron gave a new speech on immigration at the Institute of Government. Cameron endorsed my call for reform, saying: 'There's a whole chapter in the citizenship handbook on British history but incredibly there are no questions on British history on the actual test ... so we're going

---

[2] After passing the citizenship test in 2009 and receiving my Indefinite Leave to Remain that December, applicants for naturalization must wait at least one year before applying for British citizenship and the process time was an average of six months. This explains why passing the test in 2009 did not mean my becoming a citizen until about two years later.

[3] See BBC Radio 4, 'You and yours'.

[4] Since 2011, I was told by broadcasters on multiple occasions that they sought to interview alongside me a Home Secretary, Immigration Minister or some other government representative to discuss my findings about why the citizenship test needed urgent revisions. None has ever agreed.

to revise the whole test and put British history and culture at the heart of it.'[5] While the speech had been a planned major event, the insertion of a commitment to reforming the test and taking on board my critical recommendations was a significant step forward. The government planned to launch a new third edition 'by autumn 2012'.[6] I had offered to assist in refreshing the forthcoming third edition, but this was turned down. And so we waited.

The third edition test handbook was published later than scheduled on 28 January 2013 for use in tests from 25 March 2013. There were two immediate implications nowhere picked up. The first is that it gave no more than two months' notice for applicants booked to take the test on or after 25 March to prepare. Many might have been studying the second edition for their test, but this would be the wrong information for any test after late March. A longer lead-in time so prospective applicants had sufficient time to prepare would have been fairer.

From at least January to March 2013, the Home Office was publishing two very different test handbooks (the second and third editions) at the same time. Neither handbook specified when it was or was no longer applicable. Adding to the confusion, the third edition cover states it is 'The ONLY OFFICIAL handbook for the Life in the UK test' for the year '2013'.[7] However, this was patently false as all citizenship tests between 1 January and 24 March 2013 were based on the

---

[5] David Cameron, 'Prime minister's speech on immigration' (10 October 2011).

[6] This was communicated to me in a private correspondence with Ann Robertson, Policy Leader on Migration Policy in the Home Office, letter dated 14 November 2011. See also Damian Green MP, 'British nationality', House of Commons debate, 22 November 2011, column 248. Green's statement that the new test would be launched in autumn 2012 was reiterated in the House of Lords by Lord Henley, 'British Citizenship', 31 July 2012, column 0.

[7] See Home Office, *Third Edition*, cover.

second edition instead. The third edition came with its own 'official' question and answer book as seen originally with the second edition. This also says it is the 'official practice questions' for 2013 despite not being applicable until 25 March 2013 like the third edition test.[8] There was also a new 'Official Study Guide' for the first time: essentially, a condensed version of the test handbook. Likewise, this too claimed to be 'The OFFICIAL study guide' for 2013 on its cover, when it was only relevant for tests from 25 March 2013.[9]

In sum, there were three official Home Office publications all claiming to be relevant for all of 2013 when, in fact, they were relevant only from late March. Either no one had noticed this or did not much care. There is no doubt that at least some of the nearly 13,000 tests sat each month in 2013 were taken by individuals using the wrong official books, either studying the third edition for a second edition test until late March or using the second edition handbook for the third edition test after late March.

Moreover, successive test handbooks had been stating *A Journey to Citizenship* on the first and second edition covers. While the 'Life in the UK' test is regularly referred to as 'the citizenship test', this status was complicated somewhat by the requirement that permanent residents had to pass the test since the second edition in 2007. The third edition handbook is clear that it is the source of information for the 'Life in the UK' test, but it changed its subtitle to *A Guide for New Residents*. Perhaps

---

[8] See Michael Mitchell, *Life in the United Kingdom: Official Practice Questions and Answers* (London: The Stationery Office, 2013) (hereafter, 'Mitchell, *Third Edition: Practice Questions*').

[9] See Jenny Wales, *Life in the United Kingdom: Official Study Guide* (London: The Stationery Office, 2013) (hereafter, 'Wales, *Third Edition: Study Guide*'). Wales is also the author of several other books on British citizenship for Edexcel. See Jenny Wales, *Citizenship Today – Student's Book: Endorsed by Edexcel, 3rd edition* (London: Collins, 2009) and *Collins Revisions – GCSE Citizenship for Edexcel* (London: Collins, 2010).

the test should be rebranded as the UK *Permanent Residency* test as a more accurate depiction. The change from *Citizenship* to *New Residents* will have undoubtedly confused those looking for information about a citizenship test. Nor does it help that the cover refers to the status of 'new residents' and 'permanent resident' when the legal pathway referred to is instead called 'Indefinite Leave to Remain'. This terminology is nowhere mentioned in the third edition handbook. Either this was an oversight as part of a rushed job or this was an intended change meant to reduce successful applications. Either way, the third edition makes every impression of a rushed effort and preventive barrier for prospective new citizens as part of the Home Office's new strategy under then Home Secretary Theresa May of a 'hostile environment'.

The effects of introducing the new test handbook are clear. The number of tests sat in 2013 spiked by 50 per cent in March, weeks before the 25th, from 15,737 in February to 23,011 in March, before crashing to a then record low take-up of 7,426 tests sat in April, which did not pick up again until the autumn.[10] Likewise, at least 10,000 or more were passing the test each month since at least January 2010 rising to a high of 19,734 in March 2013 before crashing to a then record low of 5,207 in April and only rarely at 10,000 or above for years afterwards.[11] Complaints also appear to have been sky high. We know the test provider – PSI Services Ltd (formerly Learn Direct) – has paid out a total of £150,966 in refunds between 1 March 2014 and 3 June 2020.[12] This was paid out for 3,052 refund requests – of about £50 each, which is the full cost of

---

[10] See Baroness Williams of Trafford, 'British nationality: assessments', House of Lords debate, 23 October 2017, UNIN HL1793.

[11] See Baroness Williams of Trafford, 'British nationality: assessments', House of Lords debate, 23 October 2017, UIN HL1794.

[12] See Kevin Foster, 'British nationality: assessments', House of Commons debate, 21 June 2020, UIN 73099.

sitting the test.[13] There were 3,785 complaints made during this period.[14] Curiously, when a similar question was put to the government's front bench in the House of Lords a few weeks later, the official reply was 'the information is not readily available and could only be obtained at disproportionate cost'.[15] Both official replies can't be correct.

The test seems designed to make more fail. It can be sat no more than once every seven days until it is passed. The most attempts before passing by a single applicant had been 64.[16] At £50 per test, this would have cost £3,200. Recently, it was revealed by Kevin Foster, the Immigration Minister, that the new record for the most attempts by a single applicant is 118 during 2015 and 2016.[17] (I note that this cannot be strictly correct: taking the test no more frequently than once per seven days between 1 January 2015 and 31 December 2016 is 104 weeks – and so 104 attempts maximum allowed under the rules. Either the rules were allowed to be breached or the time frame is somewhat longer by at least an additional three months.) This would have cost £5,900 for the test only. Both examples appear to be exclusively third-edition test takers. The 'vast majority' are reported to pass by their third attempt.[18]

Despite its delayed launch, the third edition is another rushed job. The publication of the two supplemental texts was delayed. The government claimed this was because the Stationery Office needed extra time 'to check the content of these companion

---

[13] See Kevin Foster, 'British nationality: assessments', House of Commons debate, 21 July 2020, UIN 73098.

[14] Ibid.

[15] See Baroness Williams of Trafford, 'British nationality: assessments', House of Lords debate, 9 October 2017, UIN HL1746.

[16] See James Brokenshire, 'British nationality: assessments', House of Commons debate, 2 July 2015, UIN 3777.

[17] See Kevin Foster MP, 'British nationality: assessments', House of Commons debate, 8 February 2021, UIN 144733.

[18] Ibid.

products against the official handbook *after its publication*.[19] It is unclear why these could not be prepared while the handbook was approved and cleared for publication so that the three – the test handbook, the practice question book and official study guide – could appear together. However, it is clear that this meant that anyone scheduled to take the new test in March 2013 had less time to find out if the passing score was the same as before and what the question formats looked like.

It is noteworthy that the supplemental texts are not well synchronized either. Each lists sample practice questions and provides answers, but using different formats. The *Official Study Guide* refers readers to information by page numbers in the test handbook. In contrast, the *Practice Questions* refers to chapters and page numbers. This is especially confusing as the practice questions for both books were written by the same author, Michael Mitchell. It is surprising the official sample questions are not presented in the same, consistent way.

Another example of this being a rushed job was that mistakes were not only on its cover, but in its pages. For example, as noted earlier, the test claims the denominations of currency go up to £50 notes and no higher. This is untrue as there is a £100 bank note issued by the Bank of Scotland, RBS and Clydesdale Bank.[20] Confusingly, the test handbook says 'Northern Ireland and Scotland have their own banknotes', but it does not say there is any variation in denominations – only a 'UK currency', which does not take stock of differences within the UK.[21] A second example concerns the former Prime Minister Margaret Thatcher. Sadly, she died on 8 April 2013 – only two weeks after the new test was launched. But without any update since its launch, the current official test handbook of facts to

---

[19] Lord Taylor of Holbeach, 'British citizenship', House of Lords debate, 22 April 2013, column 354.

[20] See Home Office, *Third Edition*, 74; Blackstock, 'Scots immigrants left confused'.

[21] See Home Office, *Third Edition*, 74.

be memorized to become naturalized claim Thatcher remains alive despite having passed away almost a decade ago.[22] There are also typographical errors.[23] When questioned about what steps were being taken to validate the accuracy of information on the test, the government claimed 'best endeavours' were being undertaken to ensure 'a thorough quality assurance process'.[24] Clearly, this was not thorough enough.

My favourite example of what I described as an ugly question in the second test concerned how to acquire a National Insurance number. The third edition changes the information to be learned, but remains problematic. The test handbook now says: 'if you have permission to work in the UK, you will need to telephone the Department for Work and Pensions (DWP) to arrange to get a National Insurance number'.[25] However, applicants might have instead phoned Jobcentre Plus to acquire a number, which was the recommended option on the GOV.UK website (and made no mention of the DWP option).[26] This is currently done online, which is not mentioned in the test handbook as it has not been updated since 2013 to reflect this change.[27]

The rush to publication was not because of any delay due to public consultation. Once again, the government – this time the coalition government in office between 2010 and 2015 – failed to consult with anyone. But for the first time also the government does not appear to have used any independent advice. Whereas previously experts like Crick and others were

---

[22] Ibid, 57.

[23] See 'Shall I Compare Thee to a Summer's Day?' incorrectly included without its question mark. Ibid, 30.

[24] See Lord Taylor of Holbeach, 'British citizenship', House of Lords debate, 25 February 2013, column 198.

[25] Home Office, *Third Edition*, 152.

[26] See Brooks, *The 'Life in the United Kingdom' Citizenship Test*, 34.

[27] See HM Government, 'Apply for a National Insurance number', https://www.gov.uk/apply-national-insurance-number.

relied on to help develop relevant content, this appears to have been neglected, creating further problems with the test handbook's content that I will make clear in what follows. We know from a House of Lords debate that the government had 'not as yet received any direct representations' in preparing the new test handbook.[28] While the government claimed 'public comment on the new handbook has been broadly positive', it has not shared what feedback it has received nor the basis for claiming the new test was received this way.[29]

Opening up the test handbook reveals a number of problems. First, the test handbook's chapters widely vary in size. These range from the one page of text for the chapter 'What is the UK?' to 54 pages of text for the chapter 'A Long and Illustrious History'.[30] This variety in size appears to reflect differences in test coverage. My analysis of the official *Practice Questions* revealed that while the shortest chapter might have one or no question on a test, the two biggest accounted for between 14 and 18 of the 24 questions.[31] It made it possible that someone could pass, earning the minimum 18 correct answers, by studying only two of the five chapters because they were each so uneven and imbalanced. Most of the chapters might be disregarded.

Second, the third edition is incomplete. The government said that 'all the information necessary to pass the test' is contained in the test handbook.[32] The handbook notes that the test 'consists of 24 questions about important aspects of life in the UK', but it does not say how many questions must be answered correctly to pass.[33] (The same is true for the *Study*

---

[28] See Lord Taylor of Holbeach, 'British citizenship', House of Lords debate, 21 May 2013, column 44.

[29] Ibid.

[30] See Home Office, *Third Edition*, 13, 15–69.

[31] Brooks, *The 'Life in the United Kingdom' Citizenship Test*, 47.

[32] Lord Taylor of Holbeach, 'British citizenship', House of Lords debate, 22 April 2013, column 354.

[33] See Home Office, *Third Edition*, 10.

Guide.) Nor does the test handbook say anything about the format of the test. The only way to learn possible formats is to purchase additional 'official' texts like the *Practice Questions* or the *Study Guide*. So, while the facts tested are in the handbook, it is silent on how they are tested and what is required to pass the test. The information necessary is, in fact, incomplete.

Third, the new test handbook was notable for greatly expanding its contents, incorporating a new chapter on British history, especially by way of text boxes and historical dates of birth and death.[34] In total, I counted about 3,000 facts including 278 historical dates across 180 pages. This was more than ever before. My analysis of interviewees and a close examination of the *Practice Questions* and *Study Guide* reveal that very few of these dates are likely to appear on any test. Most do not appear on any test. The rare examples of dates that may appear on a test include facts like the year women first received the right to vote (1918),[35] the last year England was successfully invaded (1066)[36] and the year of D–Day (1944).[37] From what is reported and can be analysed, any test should be able to be passed even if getting dates wrong because very few appear on any test.[38] It is worth noting that the government has admitted

---

[34] Rutter notes history first tested on citizenship test in 2012, but it was not until the third edition published in January 2013 and used in tests from March 2013 that this was included. See Rutter, *Moving Up and Getting On*, 73.

[35] See Home Office, *Third Edition*, 175.

[36] Ibid, 87.

[37] Ibid, 137.

[38] Because the test handbooks make clear that 'ALL parts of the handbook', including all 278 historical dates, may be the subject of questions on the citizenship test, some study guides include charts and tables for prospective applicants to use to help memorize them. See ibid, 10 and Celine Castelino, *Pass the New Life in the UK Test*, ed. Chris Taylor (London: National Institute of Adult Continuing Education, 2013): 42, 54, 76, 103–104. This is not true for all. See Red Squirrel Publishing, *Life in the UK Test Study Guide: 2020 Edition* (London: Red Squirrel Publishing, 2020).

that 'questions are no longer asked about dates', suggesting the 278 historical dates included in the test handbook for memorization need not be recollected.[39] The historical details included were widely criticized for being partisan, inaccurate and partial.[40]

While the test handbook had wider coverage, this growth was mostly a result of expanding on the test's existing content. The discussion of the Romans is a typical illustration. The first edition states:

> The Romans, who had conquered and given law and order to the whole Mediterranean world, began to expand into Britain some decades after Julius Caesar had made an exploratory foray into Britain in 55 BC. Not until the following century did they return to conquer and establish control of the entire island except Wales and the north. There was strong opposition from the native inhabitants; one great revolt is still remembered in the name of Boudicca, the Queen of the Iceni tribe in eastern England.[41]

This text was altered for the second edition, which reads:

> In 55 BC the Romans, who had an empire covering most of the Mediterranean lands, first came to Britain with Julius Caesar. Nearly a hundred years later they came back and began a conquest of all of Britain except the highlands of Scotland. There was strong opposition

---

[39] See Lord Taylor of Holbeach, 'Immigration: UK Citizenship and Nationality', House of Lords debate, 10 October 2013, column GC128.

[40] See David Edgar, 'The British history new citizens must learn: no radicals, no homosexuals, no holocaust', *The Guardian* (11 March 2013); Historical Association, 'Britain first: the official history of the United Kingdom according to the Home Office – a critical review' (11 September 2020).

[41] Home Office, *First Edition*, 18.

from the native tribes who fought to try to keep the Romans out. A famous tribal leader who fought the Romans was Boudicca, the queen of the Iceni in what is now eastern England.[42]

And now compare this passage rewritten for the third edition:

Julius Caesar led a Roman invasion of Britain in 55 BC. This was unsuccessful and for nearly 100 years Britain remained separate from the Roman Empire. In AD 43 the Emperor Claudius led the Roman army in a new invasion. This time, there was resistance from some of the British tribes but the Romans were successful in occupying almost all of Britain. One of the tribal leaders who fought against the Romans was Boudicca, the queen of the Iceni in what is now eastern England. She is still remembered today and there is a statue of her on Westminster Bridge in London, near the Houses of Parliament.[43]

The second edition mostly rewords the first edition text, but the third edition is noticeable for adding extra content. We get additional facts that can be tested, including the year Emperor Claudius invaded Britain and the location of Boudicca's statue in London. While inclusion of a history chapter as a chapter that will be tested is new for the third edition (whereas previously it was included in the text handbook but explicitly not tested), most of the areas covered are already in the first and second editions' history chapters – but with additional facts. I have seen no evidence for why or how the extra content better captures knowledge of life in the United Kingdom that earlier editions wrongly overlooked.

---

[42] Home Office, *Second Edition*, 8.
[43] Home Office, *Third Edition*, 17.

One particularly strange addition concerns the inclusion of Sake Dean Mahomet, or rather the amount of information that must be known about him and his life.[44] Anyone wanting to become a British citizen must know more facts about Mahomet than almost anyone else in the 180-page test handbook. Applicants must know his birth year (1759), where he was born (Bengal), where this was ('a region of India'), his military service (Bengal army), when he came to Britain (1782), that he went abroad and to where (Ireland), how he was married in Ireland (eloped), the name of his wife (Jane Daly), how she is described ('an Irish girl'), what year they eloped in Ireland (1786), where he moved next (England), when this was ('at the turn of the century'), that he opened a business (restaurant), the year this happened (1810), the name of the business ('the Hindoostane Coffee House'), what street it was on (George Street), what city it was located in (London), what kind of restaurant (curry house), what made it distinctive (Britain's first curry house), what else he was known for introducing to Britain ('shampooing'), what this is ('the Indian art of head massage'), who he did this with (his wife) and the year he died (1851).[45] In total, there are 23 facts. Clearly, the government thinks there is something especially significant about Mahomet given the number of facts to learn and that he is the only non-White individual noted in the history section with a textbox.

While there is no denying his important contributions to his adopted country, it is difficult to understand why there are so many facts, such as when he moved to Ireland, that his wife is described as 'an Irish girl' and the street name for his restaurant (noted today with a City of Westminster green plaque),[46] which all seem purely trivial additional facts to make the test more difficult than necessary and without improving integration. The

---

[44] Ibid, 42.

[45] Ibid.

[46] See BBC News, 'Curry house founder is honoured' (29 September 2005).

test does not say the restaurant opened as 'the Hindoostane Dinner and Hooker Smoking Club', that Mahomet sold the business within a year of opening and became bankrupt the year afterwards, and that later he was a 'shampooing surgeon' to both King George IV and King William IV.[47]

When we look closely at the test handbook's contents, we find a number of serious problems. The first is it has become largely impractical. The original editions claimed to be handbooks that were 'a compendium of useful information helpful to those new arrivals settling in to this country'[48] or to 'increase your knowledge of British life and institutions'.[49] The third edition claims its 'hope' that readers might find its contents 'useful and interesting'.[50] But it also says the third edition will help migrants to 'integrate into society and play a full role in your local community'.[51]

Curiously, what was *removed* from the test is as problematic as what was put in – and much of what was removed seems especially essential to integrating as an engaged, active citizen. For example, the UK citizenship no longer requires that migrants know how to register with a GP, contact an ambulance or report a crime. The NHS is only mentioned once and in the history chapter, not the following chapter on modern British society.[52] Applicants do not need to know any longer the kinds of educational qualifications available nor the subjects taught in school curricula. The test went from testing *trivia* in the first and second editions to covering more of the *trivial* in the third edition.

In their place, the government has introduced new facts to be memorized. These include knowing the approximate age

---

[47] See Sejal Sukhadwala, 'The story of London's first Indian restaurant', *Londinist* (January 2019).

[48] Home Office, *First Edition*, 10.

[49] Home Office, *Second Edition*, iii.

[50] Home Office, *Third Edition*, 162.

[51] Ibid, 7.

[52] The terms NHS, GP, health and healthcare are not included in the index either. Ibid, 60, 172–180.

of Big Ben ('over 150 years')[53] and the height of the London Eye in both feet and metres ('443 feet' and '135 metres').[54] It is difficult to see how or why knowing these facts is more essential to becoming a British citizen and playing an active role than information cut out about education and schools, the NHS and healthcare access and policing.

When launching the new test, then Home Secretary Theresa May told Parliament that the third edition would cut out tedious and inessential information in favour of more carefully considered and essential facts. New citizens would no longer need to know 'about water meters and how to claim benefits', but rather more relevant facts for people 'to participate fully in our society'.[55] This statement was echoed by Immigration Minister Mark Harper, who claimed, when asked, that only 'mundane' information was 'stripped out' of the new test.[56]

When the government was challenged by my findings – thanks to helpful interventions from the Lord Reverend Roberts of Llandudno – it held to its official line. Parliamentary Under-Secretary of State for the Home Department, Lord Taylor of Holbeach, said:

> The Government do not share Dr Brooks' view that the handbook goes too far by including information about British culture and history at the expense of practical knowledge. ... The majority of those applying will have been in the UK for at least five years and should therefore be aware of practical matters, such as how to contact emergency services.[57]

---

[53] Ibid, 108.

[54] Ibid, 113.

[55] Theresa May, House of Commons debate, 25 March 2013, column 1277.

[56] Parkinson, 'British citizenship test "like a bad pub quiz"'.

[57] Lord Taylor of Holbeach, 'British citizenship', House of Lords debate, 23 May 2013, column 44.

So, knowing how to call the police or the subjects in the national curriculum are thought relevant, but not necessary to test, while information added to the third edition, such as how many feet tall is the London Eye, is necessary. The height of the London Eye, 443 feet, is a more important number for prospective citizens to know than how to dial 999. This distinction between information all migrants should know for active citizenship that should be tested and information all migrants should know for active citizenship but should *not* be ever tested is a dichotomy found nowhere else in any official policy document or statement since.

This official government position can only be described as false and not merely misleading, as part of a partisan cultural shift to the political right.[58] For the mundane and irrelevant information removed included how to contact emergency services or report a crime, while there is a rich abundance of genuinely mundane facts that are in the test handbook, for example: that London and Edinburgh are UK cities,[59] London is the UK's biggest city,[60] British currency includes the £1 coin and £5 bank note,[61] 25 December is Christmas Day,[62] Her Majesty the Queen is the head of state,[63] refuse bags should only be out when due for collection[64] and, my favourite unnecessary fact in the citizenship test handbook, that the United States of America is an independent country.[65] (Why any applicant for British citizenship must know America is independent from the UK is beyond me. Does anybody suspect otherwise?)

---

[58] See Alan Travis, 'UK migrants to face "patriotic" citizenship test', *The Guardian* (1 July 2012).
[59] Home Office, *Third Edition*, 72.
[60] Ibid, 73.
[61] Ibid, 74.
[62] Ibid, 79.
[63] Ibid, 121.
[64] Ibid, 154.
[65] Ibid, 43.

There is other material removed, rendering some sections incomplete. One example is education and schools. The test handbook says applicants can 'support your community' through helping in schools, such as by raising money through 'book sales, toy sales or bringing food to sell'.[66] The handbook also says that 'parents can often help in the classroom' although there is no mention of Disclosure and Barring Service (DBS) checks.[67] Nine of the 17 sentences in total about education encourage migrants – in a test aimed at their integration – to set up separate free schools: 'In England, parents and other community groups can apply to open a free school in their local area' and there is a website noted to learn more about how to do so.[68]

These 17 sentences replace the 115 sentences over four pages in the second edition. The following information was cut out as presumably more mundane than knowing Christmas Day is on 25 December or simply inessential for new active citizens to know: education in the UK is free and compulsory;[69] a parent or guardian may be prosecuted if his or her child fails to attend school;[70] there are primary and secondary schools;[71] information about how places are allocated at schools;[72] there are costs for school uniforms and gym clothes, as well as for school outings;[73] children in low-income families can receive support for covering the costs of school meals;[74] there are faith schools and independent schools;[75] differences in national

---

[66] Ibid, 155–156.
[67] Ibid, 156.
[68] Ibid, 156.
[69] Home Office, *Second Edition*, 66.
[70] Ibid.
[71] Ibid.
[72] Ibid.
[73] Ibid.
[74] Ibid.
[75] Home Office, *Second Edition*, 67.

curricula and subjects covered;[76] students in Wales learn Welsh;[77] and information about A-levels and university study.[78] All of these facts appear both practical and useful.

The government has never offered any explanation for their removal. Education and schools play a major role in the lives of so many, providing skills and creating opportunities. Limiting about half the information that new citizens must know to learning about free schools and little more is no way to promote better integration into society. At that time, free schools were high on the coalition government agenda and championed by then Education Secretary Michael Gove. Perhaps the best explanation for why free schools, but not grammar, comprehensives or universities, are mentioned is partisan to signpost a pet political project, not to advance the citizenship test's aim and purpose.[79]

Information removed about the NHS is also surprising. If the test is aimed at helping ensure new citizens can play an active role, then there are good reasons to include information about how to register with a GP. For example, immigrants are less likely to be registered.[80] A possible explanation is that new residents are unaware about how to register. If the knowledge about using the NHS was removed because the government thought it was obvious that new residents would find out anyway, this rationale is unsupported by the evidence. A more likely explanation is

---

[76] Ibid.

[77] Ibid.

[78] Ibid, 68–69.

[79] For example, appearing a few weeks before the third edition's publication, see James Meikle, 'Michael Gove in clash over free schools freedom of information requests', *The Guardian* (20 February 2013).

[80] See National Health Service, 'Improving GP registration among socially excluded groups'; Helen R. Stagg, Jane Jones, Graham Bickler and Ibrahim Abubakar, 'Poor uptake of primary healthcare registration among recent entrants to the UK: a retrospective cohort study', *British Medical Journal Open* (2012); Adam Steventon and Martin Bardsley, 'Use of secondary care in England by international immigrants', *Journal of Health Services Research and Policy* 16(2) (2011): 90–94, at 93.

the government's concern about so-called 'health tourism'. It is worth noting that immigrants to the UK use healthcare services less often than most English-born individuals.[81] Concerns about abuses are exaggerated and it would appear these omissions from the third edition are also motivated by partisan signposting of another pet political project.[82]

Not only did the test become more impractical, it was also inconsistent.[83] The first and second editions had the problem of claiming the incorrect number of MPs in Westminster as fact. The third edition tries to 'solve' this problem by no longer including this information for the test. It might be said that knowing the number of MPs in Westminster is inessential for becoming an integrated, active member of a local community. However, while the test no longer required knowledge about the number of MPs, it did continue to require knowing how many members currently sit in the regional Welsh Assembly, Scottish Parliament and Northern Ireland Assembly.[84] The best explanation that I can give for this omission is the partisan aim of the government to eventually reduce the number of MPs to 600.[85]

---

[81] See Steventon and Bardsley, 'Use of secondary care in England by international immigrants', 90–94.

[82] See Amy Sippitt, 'Health tourists: how much do they cost and who pays?' *Full Fact* (13 April 2015).

[83] One often overlooked inconsistency is the current third edition, if passed between 25 March and 31 October 2013, counted as evidence for both possession of knowledge of life in the United Kingdom *and* as possessing sufficient knowledge of English. From 1 November 2013, the same test was no longer applicable as evidence of possessing sufficient English. One minute the text satisfies two areas, the next it does not – and arbitrarily as the language level of the test was sufficiently high. See Home Office, *Third Edition*, 9.

[84] Ibid, 136.

[85] See Elise Uberoi and Neil Johnston, 'Constituency boundary reviews and the number of MPs', *House of Commons Library* (London: House of Commons, 8 June 2021).

Another example concerns telephone numbers. Past editions included dozens of telephone numbers and websites. To my knowledge, there is no evidence that any have ever been included in any 'Life in the UK' test. This is supported by no interviewee from over 200 I have spoken to having seen this on a test and that neither practice question and answer texts include any such questions.[86] The first edition includes 31 telephone numbers and 49 websites. This is reduced overall in the second edition to 36 telephone numbers and 23 websites. The third edition contains only five telephone numbers and 34 websites – and the numbers included are revealing. It should be noted that the test handbook is explicit: 'questions are based on ALL parts of the handbook' and no fact in the book is off-limits for any test.[87] It is not unreasonable to understand this official pronouncement to mean that telephone numbers listed in the handbook are possible facts that might be found on a test – although given what is known from widespread interviews this official pronouncement is factually untrue and no phone number does appear, in fact, to be included on any test.

The third edition takes the trouble to include five telephone numbers. The first is the National Domestic Violence Hotline (0808 200 0247).[88] The second is the HMRC self-assessment hotline (0845 300 0627).[89] The other three are for the House of Commons (0207 729 3000), Holyrood (0131 348 5200) and the Welsh Assembly (0845 010 5500).[90] The test handbook appears to forget to include Stormont (0289 052 1810), providing only a website.[91] The reason for providing telephone

---

[86] See Home Office, *Second Edition: Study Guide*; Home Office, *Third Edition: Practice Questions*.

[87] Home Office, *Third Edition*, 10.

[88] Ibid, 149.

[89] Ibid, 151.

[90] Ibid, 126 and 136. The test handbook also gives the street address for the House of Commons. See ibid, 126.

[91] Ibid, 136.

numbers is so applicants can 'book tickets' to 'visit' these institutions.[92] It is never explained – either in the test handbook or anywhere else – how or why knowing the telephone number by rote to arrange an in-person visit to Westminster and all regional governments is essential knowledge to becoming a citizen. Neither 999 or 111 are telephone numbers thought necessary for permanent residents or citizens to know.

There are various inconsistencies relating to legal institutions. Applicants are required to know about Magistrates Courts, Justice of the Peace Courts, Sheriff Courts, Youth Courts and County Courts.[93] They are not required to be aware that there is a Supreme Court in the UK. While there is broad opposition to this body among grassroot members of the Conservative Party following high-profile government defeats in 2019, it is unclear why the Supreme Court was thought unnecessary, but not other courts included, for the test in 2013.[94]

The test handbook say that the Home Secretary is 'responsible for crime' and for 'policing'.[95] Later in the same chapter, the handbook states that publicly elected Police and Crime Commissioners (PCCs) 'are responsible for the ... police force', including the appointment of local Chief Constables.[96] There is no mention of the relationship between these two roles with respect to the police. While there is information about 'examples of criminal laws', such as smoking in a public place, there is no mention about how to report a crime.[97] Nor is there mention of the rights individuals have upon arrest. There is no clear rationale for why this information is thought unnecessary and inessential.

---

[92] Ibid.

[93] Ibid, 144–147.

[94] See *The Times*, 'Half of grassroots Tories would abolish Supreme Court', *The Times* (10 October 2019).

[95] See Home Office, *Third Edition*, 127.

[96] Ibid, 142.

[97] Ibid, 140–141.

There are inconsistencies in the use of quotations. The third edition includes several quotations from plays and poetry, such as famous passages in the writings of William Shakespeare,[98] the poetry of Rudyard Kipling[99] and other poets.[100] However, it is only the quotations from three speeches from former Prime Minister Winston Churchill – all made in the same year of 1940 – that are presented in **bold** typeface.[101] It has never been said how and why only these remarks should receive special attention given to no other figure quoted throughout British history. On the face of it, this would appear to represent another example of partisan and perhaps populist influence, in this case signposting a favoured political hero of the ruling party, with no evidentiary support that these quotes have a greater importance than any other for acquiring British citizenship.

This is further confirmed by the test handbook's claim that Churchill 'was voted the greatest Briton of all time by the public'.[102] Churchill receives the most treatment of any historical figure in the handbook in terms of column inches. This claim about the public vote might suggest that this verdict is representative of the people and perhaps the pride of place that Churchill enjoys historically. There is no doubt that he remains hugely popular and widely respected by many today.

A closer scrutiny of the claim that Churchill was voted 'the greatest Briton' raises serious concerns that have gone unnoticed. It is noticeable that this test handbook published in 2013 qualifies this claim about Churchill by pointing out the vote was in 2002.[103] The handbook says nothing about this vote or its importance. But if we look at what happened in 2002,

---

[98] Ibid, 30.

[99] Ibid, 52.

[100] Ibid, 99–100.

[101] Ibid, 57.

[102] Ibid. While not included in Wales, *Third Edition: Study Guide*, it is noted as a question in Mitchell, *Third Edition: Practice Questions*, 57.

[103] See Home Office, *Third Edition*, 57.

we see this claim about a public vote refers to a short series of BBC television programmes.[104] The BBC pre-selected ten individuals each championed by a different celebrity. The vote was by telephone where the public was charged for each vote – and could vote as often as they could pay to do it. All proceeds raised went to fund a permanent memorial for the winner. The celebrity championing Churchill was former Northern Ireland Secretary Dr Mo Mowlam. Isambard Kingdom Brunel came second and Diana, Princess of Wales came third. While the test handbook mentions Brunel, it does not mention the late Princess of Wales.[105]

If this public vote was thought so important and representative by the government, it is unclear why some of the top figures in the contest are omitted.[106] The inclusion of Churchill as the public choice for 'greatest Briton' on the basis of a pay-to-vote pre-selected television competition in 2002 for a 2013 test betrays a deep partisan slant to including such a non-scientific, unrepresentative and unevidenced claim as historical fact – that all new citizens must know by heart, without knowing its source.

Similarly, the test handbook claims Rudyard Kipling's poem *If* 'has often been voted among the UK's favourite poems'.[107] No evidence is offered to substantiate this. When examined, it appears this also has a spurious basis arising from another BBC competition. There was one in 2009 to find Britain's favourite poet. Curiously, this was won by T.S. Eliot and Kipling did not make the top ten.[108] Oddly, the winner, Eliot, who became a British citizen in 1927 and, as a British citizen, earned the

---

[104] BBC News, 'Churchill votes greatest Briton', *BBC News* (24 November 2002).

[105] See Home Office, *Third Edition*, 48.

[106] Another example is John Lennon who came seventh but is not named in the test handbook either. The Beatles are mentioned once. Ibid, 92.

[107] Ibid, 52.

[108] BBC News, 'The nation's favourite poet result' (14 May 2009).

Nobel Prize for Literature in 1948, is not deemed important enough to be included in the test handbook as he is omitted.

When we go back further to 1995, there was an earlier BBC competition that year and *If* was selected as Britain's favourite poem.[109] It is unclear why this earlier 1995 survey merits inclusion, but not the 2009 competition – although then Education Secretary Michael Gove had pitched that he wanted schoolchildren from age five to begin learning lines of poetry with Kipling's name mentioned.[110]

Immigration Minister Kevin Foster has said the test aims to help new citizens 'to understand some of the cultural and historical references which occur in everyday conversations'.[111] Yet, I have never met anyone – including fans of Kipling's work – that makes mention of the 1995 competition daily, or even the 2009 result. Nor the BBC's 'Greatest Briton' competition of 2002. If the government thinks it is tracking everyday talk, they are talking to the wrong people – the justification for inclusion does not hold water.

There are other, more difficult to explain inconsistencies. One of these concerns regional dialects. Previous test handbooks have noted dialects, such as Cockney, Geordie and Scouse.[112] The third edition includes a chapter subtitle 'Languages and dialects' which states that 'the English language has many accents and dialects'.[113] For no apparent reason, the current handbook does not say what they are and there is no mention of any specific dialects. It is unclear why this

---

[109] See *The Independent*, 'Rudyard Kipling's "If" voted nation's favourite poem' (13 October 1995).

[110] See Macer Hall, 'Now Michael Gove wants pupils aged five to learn poetry', *Daily Express* (11 June 2012).

[111] See Kevin Foster, 'British nationality: assessments', House of Commons debate, 15 October 2020, UIN 102176.

[112] See Home Office, *First Edition*, 52; Home Office, *Second Edition*, 37; Home Office, *Second Edition: Study Guide*, 38, 43, 45.

[113] Home Office, *Third Edition*, 74.

information was seen as important before, why it is deemed still important to know there are various dialects, but no longer important to know any examples.[114]

There are also other unnecessary inconsistencies concerning the test handbook and its supplemental texts. The second test handbook was published with a question and answer book called the new *Official Citizenship Study Guide* with the words 'Study Guide' in larger font.[115] When the third test handbook was published, it had a supplemental question and answer book but this was called the *Official Practice Questions and Answers* book.[116] There was also an *Official Study Guide*, but this was very different from the second edition's *Study Guide* as the new *Official Study Guide* contained information from both the test handbook and the *Practice Questions* book.[117] This confusion between what a study guide is for one version versus the next is unnecessary and avoidable.

The new *Official Study Guide* is itself unclear and problematic about its usefulness. It states that it is 'designed to be used with' the official handbook.[118] The *Study Guide* says it 'offers a summary of the content' to help readers 'learn the material' needed to pass the UK citizenship test.[119] While there is no additional information in the *Study Guide* not already found in the test handbook, there are some differences, such as the *Study Guide* includes a photo of the chamber of the House of

---

[114] A second difficult to explain inconsistency concerns photo credits. Both the third edition and the *Official Study Guide* reproduce photos of places like the Giant's Causeway and the Lake District, but only the *Official Study Guide* provides any acknowledgement of photographic credits. See Wales, *Third Edition: Study Guide*, 5, 101; Home Office, *Third Edition*, 111, 116.

[115] See Home Office, *Second Edition: Study Guide*.

[116] See Mitchell, *Third Edition: Practice Questions*.

[117] See Wales, *Third Edition: Study Guide*.

[118] Ibid, 7.

[119] Ibid, 8.

Lords not found in the handbook.[120] Only the test handbook contains all the information on which citizenship tests are based. The *Study Guide* has only some of them and so is an inadequate study guide to passing tests, unless the government is secretly basing 18 or more of the 24 questions on the more limited content of the *Study Guide*.[121] This is doubtful and nowhere claimed on or off the record.

It is therefore unclear why the government has decided to publish an incomplete guide for taking the citizenship test as the 'official' *Study Guide*. Given its status, I have spoken to several applicants – all of whom have passed the test – who bought and studied only the *Study Guide* and not the longer, more complex and expensive test handbook. No doubt the government would be aware that many would risk taking the test based only on the *Study Guide*. If it was an attempt to increase the failure rate, I have seen no official data collected to confirm it and, from my own research into test applicants, this has not materialized notwithstanding this confusion.

There are also some inconsistencies between the practice questions and answers in the *Practice Questions* book and the *Official Study Guide*. For example, the latter asks: 'Which TWO things do you need to apply for UK citizenship or permanent residency?' The correct answers are: 'An understanding of life in the UK' and 'To read and speak English'.[122] In contrast, the *Practice Questions* book asks: 'To apply for UK citizenship or permanent residency, which TWO things do you need?' Its correct answers are: 'An ability to speak and read English'

---

[120] Ibid, 116.

[121] One such example is the *Official Study Guide* claims applicants should try to learn 'famous lines' by writers like Browning, Byron, Blake and Owen, but does not say which should be learned. (Ibid, 99.) The lines to be learned by each are given in the test handbook. (See Home Office, *Third Edition*, 99–100.)

[122] Wales, *Third Edition: Study Guide*, 147. The incorrect answers are 'a knowledge of maths and science' and 'access to a computer'.

and 'A good understanding of life in the UK'.[123] Several other questions and answers are similar between these two texts.[124] It is unclear why these inconsistencies appear between the texts, especially since the questions and answers for both have the same author.[125] These differences might only confuse applicants on what to study, if they have purchased the three official texts for the third edition.

Gender imbalance is a particular problem with the third edition. The Home Office's triumphant press release announcing the new test noted the 'people that have shaped Britain' included in the handbook. It listed the names of nine men and no women – and a poignant example of the test's woman problem.[126] Undoubtedly, women are far less visible than men in the test handbook. There are 29 men, but only four women (Florence Nightingale, Emmeline Pankhurst, Margaret Thatcher, Mary Peters) listed with dates of birth or death in the test handbook's history chapter.[127] Neither of Her Majesty the Queen's birthdays are mentioned – nor that she has two birthdays, in a royal tradition that stems back to 1748 during the reign of King George II, which are her actual day of birth and an 'official' birthday celebration combined with Trooping the Colour.[128]

There are other women mentioned in the handbook's history chapter, but mostly as the wives of more important husbands.[129]

---

[123] Mitchell, *Third Edition: Practice Questions*, 124. The incorrect answers are 'a UK bank account' and 'a driving licence'.

[124] Ibid, 123, 128 and Wales, *Third Edition: Study Guide*, 77, 80.

[125] This is Michael Mitchell. His name is on the cover of *Practice Questions* and his writing questions for the *Study Guide* is acknowledged in ibid, 5.

[126] It would be interesting to know if any women were involved in drafting the third edition handbook.

[127] See Home Office, *Third Edition*, 49, 51, 66, 67.

[128] See Sabrina Barr, 'Why does the queen have two birthdays?' *The Independent* (12 June 2021).

[129] The one exception is Her Majesty the Queen. See Home Office, *Third Edition*, 121.

The more commonly found examples include monarchs, such as the wives of King Henry VII, King Henry VIII and William of Orange.[130] Sake Dean Mahomet, the founder of Britain's first curry house, is the only non-monarch whose wife is named (Jane Daly). Prospective applicants are required to know Mahomet moved to Ireland and eloped with Daly.[131] There is no one example of eloping in British history that must be known other than this. All other women noted are queens, such as Boudicca,[132] Mary, Queen of Scots,[133] Queen Elizabeth I[134] and Queen Anne.[135]

Eleven men and six women are noted in sport and culture, as well as three women for being authors and writers.[136] There are no female musicians, artists or poets noted; but there seven male musicians, nine male artists, six male authors or writers and five male poets listed.[137] This adds up to 38 men and only 9 women.

The gender imbalance throughout the test handbook is exacerbated by several surprising omissions. The third edition removes previously included information about childcare, maternity leave and schools. This is mitigated by the inclusion of information about laws against discrimination on the basis of several factors, including sex, pregnancy, sexuality and marital status.[138] There is also information included about domestic violence, female genital mutilation and forced marriage.[139]

Some of the strangest – and most clearly politically motivated – changes made to the test handbook concern its

---

[130] Ibid, 25, 27, 36–37.

[131] Ibid, 42.

[132] Ibid, 17.

[133] Ibid, 28–29.

[134] Ibid, 28–29, 31.

[135] Ibid, 38–39.

[136] Ibid, 84–100.

[137] Ibid. Surprisingly, there is no mention of L.S. Lowry.

[138] Ibid, 149.

[139] Ibid, 149–150.

glossary. The second edition introduced a glossary at its end. This contained 413 terms over 31 pages.[140] Glossary terms noted included 'Bank Holiday',[141] 'devolution',[142] 'first past the post'[143] and 'liberty'.[144] Other terms retained in the third edition include: 'civil service',[145] 'constituency',[146] 'Houses of Parliament',[147] 'to go on strike',[148] 'terrorism'[149] and 'volunteer'.[150] Some retained terms are listed without the capital letters they had in the second edition (such as 'bank holiday' instead of Bank Holiday)[151] or with capital letters they did *not* have in the second edition (such as 'General Election' instead of general election).[152] Such inconsistencies seem to be another example of a rushed job.

The third edition significantly cuts the glossary's size to 110 entries over only seven pages, a reduction of nearly three-quarters.[153] The 303 glossary terms removed for the third edition include: 'academic course',[154] 'ante-natal care',[155] 'assessment methods (education)',[156] 'asylum',[157] 'bursary',[158]

---

[140] See Home Office, *Second Edition*, 114–145.
[141] Ibid, 117.
[142] Home Office, *Third Edition*, 124.
[143] Ibid, 127.
[144] Ibid, 132.
[145] Ibid, 165.
[146] Ibid, 166.
[147] Ibid, 167.
[148] Ibid, 169.
[149] Ibid, 170.
[150] Ibid.
[151] Ibid, 164.
[152] Ibid, 166.
[153] Ibid, 164–170.
[154] Home Office, *Second Edition*, 116.
[155] Ibid.
[156] Ibid, 117.
[157] Ibid.
[158] Ibid, 119.

'code of practice',[159] 'contraception',[160] 'disability',[161] 'discrimination',[162] 'divorce',[163] 'emergency services',[164] 'free press',[165] 'harassment',[166] 'higher education',[167] 'immigration',[168] 'legal aid',[169] 'L-plates',[170] 'maternity leave',[171] 'mental illness',[172] 'mortgage',[173] 'outpatient',[174] 'paternity leave',[175] 'pressure group',[176] 'racially-motivated crime',[177] 'sick pay',[178] 'torture',[179] 'tuition fees',[180] 'victim'[181] and 'welfare benefits'[182] among others. Most of these excluded terms relate to education, healthcare, housing and rights. Their removal seems politically motivated, like these are everyday rights and responsibilities the government wants to hide from, not provide further support for, prospective new citizens – all part of a longstanding pattern since the Tory-led coalition government was launched. Why else remove any mention of

[159] Ibid, 121.
[160] Ibid, 122.
[161] Ibid, 124.
[162] Ibid.
[163] Ibid, 125.
[164] Ibid, 127.
[165] Ibid, 128.
[166] Ibid.
[167] Ibid, 129.
[168] Ibid, 130.
[169] Ibid, 132.
[170] Ibid.
[171] Ibid, 133.
[172] Ibid.
[173] Ibid, 134.
[174] Ibid, 135.
[175] Ibid, 136.
[176] Ibid, 138.
[177] Ibid, 139.
[178] Ibid, 142.
[179] Ibid, 143.
[180] Ibid, 144.
[181] Ibid.
[182] Ibid.

legal aid, harassment and racially motivated crime unless the government wanted to make it more difficult for migrants to learn about them? Even if we questioned their original inclusion, they were already listed. Their deletion was not by accident and, taken together, there appears a theme of a test that is an unwelcoming barrier.

The third edition introduces several new glossary terms. These include: 'civil war',[183] 'House (history)' defined as 'a family (for example the House of York)',[184] 'illegal',[185] 'medieval/Middle Ages',[186] 'Pale (history)',[187] 'Protestants',[188] 'rural',[189] 'sonnet'[190] and '*The Phone Book*'.[191] There is no evidence available for how or why glossary terms were selected for removal or inclusion and what relevance it has on ensuring test applicants who understand these terms have acquired a sufficient knowledge of life in the United Kingdom. Again, much of these changes seem driven by partisan pursuits rather than any clear, evidenced and objective basis.

The British citizenship test is the test for citizenship that few British citizens seem able to pass. I find it hard to disagree with David Blunkett, who acknowledged to me that Labour "didn't get the first test entirely right". However, the current test is "a complete dog's dinner".[192] I agree with Blunkett. The vastly expanded test bursting with trivial facts, many of which do not seem essential or find their way onto any test, has strayed further than ever from its original justifying aims

---

[183] Home Office, *Third Edition*, 165.

[184] Ibid, 167.

[185] Ibid.

[186] Ibid, 168.

[187] Ibid.

[188] Ibid, 169. Other religious affiliations are not included in the glossary, but appear in the main text. See ibid, 76–77.

[189] Ibid, 169.

[190] Ibid.

[191] Ibid, 170.

[192] Private correspondence.

and purposes. Many of the changes appear political to make citizenship a more partisan issue, and not evidenced, from the decision to require memorization of Churchill as the greatest Briton based on a non-scientific television competition nearly 20 years ago to only requiring knowledge about being able to set up a free school as a favoured pet project of that time with nothing said any longer about any other kind of school, any national curriculum and more.

Not every change was for the worse. The first welcome difference is an improved look. The first edition contains no images. The second edition is mostly black and white with few colour images. The third edition is the first test handbook to be published in full colour.[193] The handbook cover has changed from first-edition blue and second-edition purple to vibrant red (*Official Study Guide*), white (test handbook) and blue (*Practice Questions*). Inside, the third edition reads less like a policy report common to the earlier versions and more like a textbook.

The second improvement is there was a free, sample, online test offering a useful example of what the test might be like for applicants. It gives applicants 45 minutes to answer 24 questions. After the test is completed, it tells applicants whether they have passed and provides the correct answers to any incorrect guesses. This test is unofficial and for practice only. All questions offered that I have seen can be found in the *Practice Questions* book. Multiple-choice questions use a list of possible answers in the same order as found in *Practice Questions*, too. This is a very welcome change to support those interested in learning more about the citizenship test. However, it is somewhat disturbing that the government appears to use data from this one official practice test that can be taken by anyone – and as often as they like – for evidence that the test is

---

[193] An anonymous reader notes this may well have been part of an effort to highlight the 'illustrious' history of Britain, echoing chapter three ('A long and illustrious history'). See Home Office, *Third Edition*, 14–69.

fair and not overly difficult, claiming practice test takers scored 86 per cent on average.[194]

Notwithstanding these steps in the right direction, much else with the third edition has gone badly wrong. The test handbook had mistakes, inconsistencies, gender imbalance problems and more pointed out since its launch. Despite these issues being raised, the government has failed to act and buried its head in the sand, ignoring a growing crisis. And still thousands must sit and pass a test originally set by David Cameron's government that he failed on live television. A test for becoming a member of a political community based on knowledge thought essential for integrated, active inclusion ought to have some basis in fact. When the members cannot pass the test either – including those in charge of the government setting the test – this is a farce that cannot go on any longer. And it is a recipe for trouble as new citizens who pass can be shaped by this negative, exploitative experience undermining their motivation to become more involved in a community they feel wants their fees and tax income, but not their potential contribution as a welcome citizen. This was the damning indictment that I heard consistently when interviewing naturalized British citizens. Instead of ensuring integration, the badly constructed test was creating a sense of disintegration to a surprising degree. The time for change had come and continued inaction threatened to make a bad situation worse.

---

[194] It is claimed 93,000 took the practice test, but not the timeframe. See Lord Taylor of Holbeach, 'Citizenship test', House of Lords debate, 26 February 2013, column 955.

SIX

Building Bridges and a Better Test

The citizenship test has failed to achieve its original aims and purpose to ensure migrants can 'integrate into society and play a full role in your local community' as permanent residents and British citizens.[1] Shortly after the test was launched, the government was confronted with evidence of its mistakes, inconsistencies and imbalances rendering it unfit for purpose.[2] A few years later, the evidence grew that the test was not supporting integration and having a counterproductive effect.[3]

The official response from 2013 to today has been to deny there was ever a problem. Ministers claim the 'majority' of feedback they have seen is positive, but they have never offered evidence of what feedback was received.[4] There has

---

[1] Home Office, *Third Edition*, 7.

[2] See Brooks, *The 'Life in the United Kingdom' Citizenship Test*.

[3] See Brooks, *Becoming British*, chapter 4. See also Bridget Byrne, 'Testing times: the place of the citizenship test in the UK immigration regime and new citizens' responses to it', *Sociology* 51(2) (2017): 323–338; Melanie Cooke, 'Barrier or entitlement? The language and citizenship agenda in the United Kingdom', *Language Assessment Quarterly* 6(1) (2009): 71–77; Linda Morrice, 'British citizenship, gender and migration: the containment of cultural differences and the stratification of belonging', *British Journal of Sociology of Education* 38(5) (2017): 597–609; Audrey Osler, 'Testing citizenship and allegiance: policy, politics and the education of adult migrants in the UK', *Education, Citizenship and Social Justice* 4(1) (2009): 63–79.

[4] See Lord Taylor of Holbeach, 'British citizenship', House of Lords debate, 21 May 2013, column 44.

never been an official review or consultation since the test launch in November 2005. The only apparent attempt at organizing feedback is from the administrator of the test, not the Home Office. Nor is there any effort to assess whether the 'Life in the UK' test does, in fact, promote British values and improve integration.[5] It's almost like they're afraid to look as it would show how much the test has veered off course from its original justifying aims in order to serve alternative, partisan and inexplicit ends. Perhaps the government hoped no one will notice.

The government claimed it 'took into account feedback received from previous applicants and others who had provided comments on it', but did not say if this was a formal exercise or noting what is said about the test in the press and academic commentary.[6] I suspect it this was a reference to a comment made in 2013 about a 'user survey' of 664 people who took the second edition.[7] On the basis of their expressing an apparent interest – the results of this exercise have never been made public nor referenced beyond this brief comment – in having more information 'about history, government and the legal system'. And so the third edition attempted to do this, but admittedly without asking any one of them if it had succeeded in satisfying this recommendation. Worse, this is not what the third-edition handbook claims. It notes the handbook will give 'a broad general knowledge of the culture, laws and history of the UK' – adding in 'culture' and leaving out 'government'.[8] Facts like these make one wonder if ministers

---

[5]   See Baroness Williams of Trafford, 'British nationality: assessments', 9 October 2017, UIN HL1747.

[6]   See Baroness Williams of Trafford, 'British nationality: assessments', House of Lords debate, 23 October 2017, UIN HL1747.

[7]   See Lord Taylor of Holbeach, 'Immigration: UK citizenship and nationality', House of Lords debate, 10 October 2013, column GC127.

[8]   See Home Office, *Third Edition*, 7.

have seen the test handbook prior to making official statements about its contents.

The only other example that comes to mind where test feedback was sought is from when the Stationery Office sent me a brief online survey via email, as it did to individuals acquiring the newly published third-edition test handbook in spring 2013. The survey asks about the purchasers' first language, the reason for deciding to live in the UK (options included 'work permit', 'student' and 'family') and the resources used to find out information.[9] While any such contact is welcome, it is inadequate. First, not everyone purchasing the handbook is an immigrant and planning to start a life in the UK. Some may be British citizens purchasing the text out of curiosity or on behalf of a spouse. Second, it was possible to provide feedback multiple times using the same link. It is unclear how representative a picture it would create.

This lack of consultation is a significant problem because it means the government lacks any official basis for determining whether the citizenship test is fit for purpose. When asked what steps have been taken 'to ensure that the Life in the UK test reflects contemporary Britain', ministers don't say, but reassure an emphasis on 'British history, culture and democracy' (and not 'culture, laws and history' as noted in the actual handbook)[10] – and not how this was done.[11] It is claimed the test is regularly updated – most recently as February 2020 – but this appears to be no more than removing test questions for applicants with no changes made to the test handbook since its publication in 2013.[12]

---

[9] Personal correspondence received 6 June 2013.

[10] See Home Office, *Third Edition*, 7.

[11] See James Brokenshire, 'British nationality: assessments', House of Commons debate, 24 November 2014, UIN 215126.

[12] See Kevin Foster, 'British nationality: assessments', House of Commons debate, 3 March 2020, UIN 20526.

If the government refuses to accept the third edition was problematic since its launch, it is irrefutable that essential changes are required – and, in one specific case, so that the test can comply with the law. In April 2014, about a year after the third edition was published, the government granted protected minority status to the Cornish. What this did is grant a new officially recognized legal status to the Cornish. As signatory to the Framework Convention for the Protection of National Minorities in 1995 and ratified in 1998, the UK was under an obligation to combat discrimination, promote equality, preserve and develop the culture and identity of its officially recognized minority groups.[13] The UK remains a signatory post-Brexit.[14] The Welsh, Scots and Irish are already officially protected minority groups.

Then Chief Secretary to the Treasury Danny Alexander hailed this as a significant 'commitment' including new funding to support the promotion of the Cornish language.[15] This funding support has continued since.[16] Yet other than additional funds to preserve the Cornish language and related cultural activities, the wider consequences of this new legal status seemed elusive.[17]

It seems clear that the government did not think through these implications fully. One problem arising from Census 2021 is that Cornish was excluded, but not the other protected minorities.[18] This appears to be a breach of ensuring the

---

[13] See CETS 157 – Framework Convention for the Protection of National Minorities (coe.int).

[14] Ibid.

[15] See HM Treasury, 'Cornish granted minority status within the UK', 24 April 2014.

[16] See HM Ministry of Housing, 'New funding to preserve Cornish culture, language and heritage', 5 July 2019.

[17] See Emma Hallett, 'Will minority status help Cornwall?', BBC News (24 April 2014).

[18] See Sam Beamish, 'People urged to write Cornish as their nationality in census after tick box snub', *Cornwall Live* (3 March 2021).

Cornish are afforded the same equality as other protected minorities which should have warranted their inclusion.

A second problem is the continuing exclusion of the Cornish from the citizenship test. I raised this issue within 24 hours of the official announcement in a statement that was tagged 'Cornish pasties must be added to the test'.[19] In examining the 180-page *Third Edition* handbook, I could find only a single mention of anything Cornish or Cornwall – the Eden Project – otherwise, it is like the Cornish don't exist. What protected minority status means for the test handbook is that it must be expanded to include Cornish culture and history, Cornish food (such as the Cornish pasty), the Cornish national flower, the Cornish patron saint (St Pirin), the date of St Pirin's Day (5 March) and acknowledge the existence of the Cornish language – just as the test handbook recognizes similar facts for the Welsh, Scots and Irish. The only Cornish individual mentioned in the test handbook is *Lord of the Flies* author William Golding, but he is not identified as being from Cornwall which must be corrected. Other notable figures for possible inclusion might be Captain William Bligh, the scientist Sir Humphrey Davy, chef Rick Stein and actor John Nettles. Whoever or whatever is included should be a product of public consultation, but the need to make inclusions is required and urgent.

Parliamentary written questions rarely receive interesting replies from ministers who seem overly eager to draw a line under any and every possible criticism. Perhaps the most bizarre that I have seen since advising on what to ask the government is about the protected minority status of the Cornish. Baroness Smith of Basildon asked the government in 2017 about what changes they were planning to make to the citizenship test in light of the fact that the Cornish were granted protected

---

[19] See Thom Brooks, 'Cornish pasties must be added to the UK citizenship test', *The Conversation* (25 April 2014).

minority status. We were looking for some acknowledgement that the government understood the need to consult on a new test handbook which included at least some information about Cornish. But instead there was the most extraordinary reply that the government claimed it would, as a result of the Cornish having this status, look at introducing the test in Cornish.[20] This would follow given the test is available in Welsh and Scots Gaelic, but it goes far beyond putting Cornish facts in the test by putting the test into Cornish. Four years later and there has been nothing forthcoming on developments since. This must change.

While the government occasionally tries to brush off criticisms as motivated by party affiliation, this is not a party political issue nor should it ever be.[21] This book levels criticisms wherever it is warranted and not only at tests launched by Labour or the Conservative–Liberal Democrat coalition. Citizenship should be an inherently non-partisan issue if it is to capture what all citizens have in common and my recommended reforms include ensuring partisanship plays no part in designing the next citizenship test. Calls for the test's revision and relaunch are cross-party and across political aisles.[22] Politicians from most mainstream parties can be found in agreement that the current test must change.[23]

---

[20] See Baroness Williams of Trafford, 'British nationality: assessments', House of Lords debate, 24 October 2017, UIN HL1872.

[21] See Lord Parkinson of Whitley Bay, 'UK citizenship: history', House of Lords debate, 14 April 2021, column 1274 ('The noble Baroness mentioned another academic. I understand that Professor Brooks is an advisor to the Labour Party. He has certainly made his representations on the citizenship test well known').

[22] See House of Lords, 'UK citizenship: history', House of Lords debate, 14 April 2021, columns 1272–1275; British Future, *Barriers to Britishness: Report of the Alberto Costa Inquiry into Citizenship Policy* (London: British Future, 2020).

[23] One possible exception is the Scottish National Party (SNP). The evidence is found in their blueprint for Scotland's independence

There is an opportunity *now* to act on this cross-party support to introduce the urgent and necessary changes required to the test. This follows from the significant work of the House of Lords Select Committee on Citizenship and Civic Engagement. In 2018, this committee published the most impressive report I have seen on the topic to date for any jurisdiction.[24] The Report makes several important recommendations, including: renaming 'Fundamental British Values' as 'Shared Values of British Citizenship' to openly acknowledge these values are shared with people from other countries; creating a statutory entitlement to citizenship education (albeit stopping short of stating this must mean including citizenship tests in secondary schools); a new Advisory Group should be constituted to review the content of the citizenship test as part of a public consultation; and there should be a review of citizenship ceremonies with a view to providing greater publicity and impact.[25]

Since the committee's report was published, one of the committee's most prominent members, David Blunkett, has called repeatedly on the government to act on its recommendations.[26] The government minister assured him

---

during the 2013 referendum. The SNP government makes clear that, if successful, an independent Scotland would not have a citizenship test. This is because it would seek to encourage more migration and is concerned that the test is mostly used as a barrier. From what evidence I have gathered, this claim that the test has become more a barrier than a bridge is confirmed. See Scottish Government, *Scotland's Future: Your Guide to an Independent Scotland* (Edinburgh: Scottish Government, 2013): 495–496.

[24] See House of Lords Select Committee on Citizenship and Civic Engagement, *The Ties That Bind: Citizenship and Civic Engagement in the 21st Century* (London: House of Lords, 2018) (HL Paper 118) (hereafter 'House of Lords, *The Ties That Bind*').

[25] Ibid, 123–124, 129.

[26] Lord Blunkett, 'British citizenship', House of Lords debate, 3 October 2019, column 1779 and Lord Blunkett, 'Life in the UK test', House of Lords debate, 3 November 2020, column 628.

that she would, as she was concerned the test was morphing into *Trivial Pursuit*.[27] Yet, still the government has done nothing and could not say, when asked, what assessment had been done to ensure the procedure for becoming British was effective.[28] Things are now farcical with the government repeatedly claiming all is well while acknowledging it makes no effort to discern whether this is true. It is now widely acknowledged, as Blunkett has said, that the test is based on what can only be described as an 'extraordinarily out-of-date booklet'.[29] The government acknowledged the test 'obviously needs a little attention'.[30] It was claimed recently that a new fourth edition is to be launched in 2022.[31] But what steps are being taken to do what by who and why are all unknown. This should raise serious concerns that the problems plaguing the third edition since its launch are likely to repeated.

An overarching problem is that, over the course of its three editions, the test has become more and more of a *barrier*.[32] Crossbench Peer Lord Singh of Wimbledon wryly observes the test 'is a bit of an obstacle course'.[33] He is correct. This is a concern because new citizens become part of a community to

---

[27] Baroness Williams of Trafford, 'British citizenship', House of Lords debate, 3 October 2019, column 1780. See also Baroness Williams of Trafford, 'British nationality: assessments', House of Lords debate, 29 March 2019, UIN HL14599.

[28] See Lord Dubs, 'British citizenship', House of Lords debate, 3 October 2019, column 1778.

[29] See Lord Blunkett, 'Integrated communities', House of Lords debate, 15 March 2018, column 1776.

[30] See Lord Bourne of Aberystwyth, 'Integrated communities', House of Lords debate, 15 March 2018, column 1776.

[31] See Baroness Williams of Trafford, 'British nationality: assessments', House of Lords debate, 7 December 2020, UIN HL10607.

[32] See Thom Brooks, 'The "Life in the UK" test has morphed into a barrier to immigration', *New Statesman* (16 July 2013).

[33] Lord Singh of Wimbledon, 'Life in the UK test', House of Lords debate, 3 November 2020, 628.

which they belong and make a contribution, not on account of only jumping through hoops.

It is undeniable that the mere use of citizenship tests has some barrier-like effects in lowering the number of applications. This is not unique to the UK. Studies have found similar effects in different test models in Germany and the Netherlands, too.[34] Perhaps this signals a shift to a more exclusionary and partisan re-conception of citizenship and the use of citizenship tests beyond the UK. However, if the aim is to help keep others out, there are more effective and efficient ways this could be done without any need of a knowledge exam like the 'Life in the UK' test. For example, the minimum income requirement could be raised, the residency requirement extended or the English language requirements made more difficult. These are all parts of the naturalization requirements and each could be more consistently and transparently applied than the time and effort in designing a 180-page test handbook with constantly evolving – and sometimes contested, if not false – information that is difficult to update frequently enough to ensure all 'correct' answers remain genuinely true for every officially authorized test.

Consider the Channel Island of Jersey. Under Jersey law, all candidates are required to hold British citizenship to stand in its States Assembly. Recently, the Assembly considered whether to create a new 'Life in Jersey' test that non-British citizens could take and, if passed, would allow them to stand for election proposed by Deputy Inna Gardiner. The rationale was this would allow individuals from countries that do not recognize dual citizenship to stand. The test would be modelled on the UK's current citizenship test. The motion was defeated by default after the Assembly split in a 22 to 22 vote with

---

[34] For example, see Ricky van Oers, *Deserving Citizenship: Citizenship Tests in Germany, the Netherlands and the United Kingdom* (Leiden: Martinus Nijhoff Publishers, 2013): 276.

critics saying that it was simply wrong to make residents living in Jersey for decades prove their worth through such a test.[35]

This perfectly illustrates that building barriers is more efficient and effective without the need for conceiving, drafting, launching and administering a multiple-choice test, if the government wanted to have such barriers in the first place. A revised and reformed citizenship test need not – and should not – be used primarily as a barrier.

In reflecting on alternative models to draw on for inspiration, these are broadly of two varieties.[36] The first is common to Continental Europe where citizenship is often learned alongside language.[37] In France, individuals applying for citizenship are interviewed to 'verify, pursuant to Article 21–24 of the Civil Code, that the applicant has in particular sufficient knowledge of French history, culture and society'.[38] Questions cover information in a 28-page *Citizens' Handbook*.[39] In Germany, individuals may apply for citizenship after eight years and renounce their current nationality, as Germany does not recognize dual nationality. All must pass a citizenship test of 33 questions scoring 17 or higher with three questions relating to whichever German state the applicant lives in. The questions cover Germany's legal system, society and living conditions.[40] The Netherlands has a civic integration diploma.[41] For each, the main hurdle for most applicants is sufficient language skills.

A second variety is where language can be less of a barrier, such as in English-speaking countries like Australia, the UK

---

[35] BBC News, 'Jersey States rejects citizenship test for non-British election candidates' (11 February 2021).

[36] See Liam Byrne, *A More United Kingdom* (London: Demos, 2008): 45–47.

[37] See Christian Joppke, *Citizenship and Immigration* (Cambridge: Polity, 2010).

[38] See French Government, *Naturalisation*.

[39] See French Ministry de l'Interieur, *Livret du Citoyen* (2015).

[40] See German Federal Ministry of the Interior and Community, *Naturalisation*.

[41] See Dutch Ministry of Justice and Security, *Civic integration for more secure residence permit and naturalization*.

and United States, where many will be exempt because their native language is English and come from an English-speaking country already. As a native of the US, I am exempt from English language requirements in the UK. Americans (and British citizens) are automatically exempt from language requirements in Australia, too. However, there is no exception in France, Germany or the Netherlands based on my dual UK–US nationality.

Australia's review and reform of citizenship law and policy two decades ago inspired similar changes in the UK. However, Australia was slightly later in launching its own test. Its review started in 2006.[42] Interestingly, Australia used the teething problems of the November 2005 launch of the UK test as a moment to learn lessons for its test introduced through the Australian Citizenship Amendment (Citizenship Testing) Act 2007.[43] In a Parliamentary Library note, it is observed that the UK test was mistaken to offer a partial view of history that should be more rounded. The note claimed that the UK test took a high-brow approach to British life, focusing on traditional institutions like the courts, the church and the Queen to the exclusion of the workplace and everyday life; and it was thought to have as one of its purposes the exclusion of individuals from becoming British.[44]

Unliked the UK where the test can only be accessed if purchased, Australia launched a test handbook that was

---

[42] Australian Government, *Australian Citizenship: Much More Than a Ceremony* (Canberra: Department of Immigration and Multicultural Affairs, 2006).

[43] Australian Citizenship Amendment (Citizenship Testing) Act 2007.

[44] See Sue Harris Rimmer, *Bills Digest: Australian Citizenship Amendment (Citizenship Testing) Bill 2007*, Parliamentary Library (Canberra: Australian Parliament, 2007): 5. Rimmer notes that humourists had been critical of an Australian test, noting 'a favourite of the author' as an example: 'Is it best to take a sick day on: (a) when the cricket's on, (b) when the cricket's on or (c) when's the cricket on?' (ibid, 8).

freely available online and easy to locate. The test included information about what it means to be an Australian citizen, noting things like a duty to vote, to work in the defence force or public service; and to serve on a jury. Test applicants must know Australian values like respect for equal worth, freedoms of speech and religion, support for democracy and the rule of law, and tolerance. There is also some information on demographics and general history. The test handbook entitled *Our Common Bond* is 49 pages.

Not everything on the Australian test has been commendable. One such example is that all applicants were formerly required to know that 'Sir Donald Bradman was the greatest cricket batsman of all time. He was small and slight but amazingly quick on his feet, playing his shots almost like a machine'.[45] While knowing that Sir Donald is a famous cricketer might be an important part of Australia's cultural history, it is much less clear that knowing he was 'small and slight … playing his shots almost like a machine' is essential for new migrants hoping to integrate as active Australian citizens. Despite having this information in the test handbook, then Prime Minister Kevin Rudd confessed that, in fact, no test had ever asked about him anyway.[46]

The new test handbook *Our Common Bond* has removed information like this. Launched in November 2020, it takes a stronger focus on 'national values'.[47] This is done through include five multiple-choice questions about the values of mutual respect, equality and democracy that must all be

---

[45] On Bradman's removal, see Reuters, 'Strewth! Australia drops cricket from citizenship test', 22 November 2008; ABC News, 'Don gets dropped from citizenship test', 21 November 2008.

[46] See News.com.au, 'Don Bradman was never in Australian citizenship test', 21 October 2009.

[47] See Mostafa Rachwani, 'The new Australian citizenship test: what is it and what has changed?' *The Guardian* (17 September 2020); Department of Home Affairs (Australian Government), *Citizenship Interview and Test*.

answered correctly – and as part of answering correctly 75 per cent or more of the overall test from the full set of 20 questions asked. The freely accessible test handbook includes sample test questions as a complete resource about the test.

Where Australia has improved is in looking towards the test used in the United States which was the first such standardized test originally launched in 1986. The main aim of the American 'civics' test is mostly symbolic. Its facts are uncontested and non-partisan. Applicants must answer correctly at least six of ten questions – with the full set of possible questions and answers available in multiple languages. For example, it can ask for the name of the first President (George Washington), who was President during the Civil War (Abraham Lincoln), the institution on top of each of the three branches of American government (President, Congress, Supreme Court), some basic geography like naming one of the two longest rivers (Mississippi, Missouri) and naming anyone of the over 2,000 Native American tribes (for example, Apache, Iroquois, Mohawk, Pequot, Sioux). The test can be sat for free if failed the first time – and all who pass can immediately swear an oath for citizenship.[48]

The test is popular with many state lawmakers. Nearly half of all US states include a requirement for receiving a high school diploma that students learn about the citizenship test. In this way, the information for becoming and being American is more normalized and brought into everyday life. The information is not for migrant eyes only, but freely and readily accessible to all.

The US test has its critics. Called 'a joke' measuring only 'rote memorization', a common complaint is that American citizens does not require any particular knowledge as most Americans are citizens by birth and lack such knowledge anyway.[49] There

---

[48] See US Citizenship and Immigration Services, 'Study for the test (2008 version)'.

[49] See Peter J. Spiro, *Beyond Citizenship: American Identity After Globalization* (Oxford: Oxford University Press, 2008): 43.

is also the contested nature of American identity. Moreover, the test questions were not always appropriate. Decades ago, the test asked more trivial questions, such as the height of the Bunker Hill Monument. There had been another question asking 'how many stars are there on a quarter?' The problem was there was more than one quarter in circulation and they had different numbers of stars.[50] Both have since been removed.

There was a brief and widely reported change during the last days of President Donald Trump's term of office where he made the test longer and more difficult.[51] The test was doubled in size (for example, applicants had to answer 20 questions instead of ten) scoring the same pass rate as before (60 per cent). The test's content was changed as well. The correct answer to the question of who US Senators represent in Congress was changed from 'all people of the state' to 'citizens in their state'. Applicants for American citizens needed to know the name of all three branches of government. Previously, they needed only to remember one. The US Citizenship and Immigration Services agency admitted that these changes 'may inadvertently create potential barriers to the naturalization process'. Despite these changes, pass rates remained high at 94 per cent.[52] Nonetheless, there were growing concerns that most US citizens could not pass the test either.[53] A few months later, after Joe Biden became President, he reversed these changes and reverted to the shorter, non-partisan test in place previously, first set in 2008.[54]

---

[50] See Simon Romero and Miriam Jordan, 'New U.S. citizenship test is longer and more difficult', *New York Times* (3 December 2020).

[51] Ibid.

[52] Abe Kwok, 'In the end, Trump's tougher citizenship test had no impact on immigrants', *Arizona Republic* (14 June 2021).

[53] CBS News, 'Most Americans could not pass a citizenship test, a major issue for the country' (19 January 2021).

[54] See Geneva Sands, 'Biden administration rolls back Trump-era citizenship civics test', *CNN* (22 February 2021).

Several lessons can be learned from the American model. First, the barriers are set up prior to the citizenship test. The test is a final and symbolic step before a citizenship ceremony. Second, the test is in plain sight. It is available freely, even in multiple languages, and all possible questions and answers can be seen in advance. This makes it transparent and accountable: citizens old and new can have confidence about its contents and their veracity. Third, the test is non-partisan – and when Trump experimented with a more partisan edge it only lasted weeks before being uncontroversially scrapped. This is important as to become a permanent citizen is joining a community of all, not just one political side of it. Finally, the information on the test is widely shared as important for *all* citizens. Several US states now teach the American citizenship test materials in schools. Knowing about these essential facts of government, history and geography is for everybody, not only migrants. And it brings people together, rather than pulling them apart. New citizens understand that other citizens will likely know this information, too. This helps build solidarity between them.

It is welcome that Australia's test appears to be taking on more and more of the American-style model. Now it is time for the UK to do the same. After leaving the European Union, it is urgent and critical that a fundamental review is undertaken into how the test should work moving forward in a new, fourth edition launched by the end of 2024. It is crucial we learn from past mistakes and take action now to improve.

The case for a new test – that is *a bridge*, not a barrier – could not be stronger. Since its original launch in 2005, the then government promised it 'will be reviewed in light of experience'.[55] Over ten years and two million tests sat later, no such review is in sight. Given exclusion is more effectively and

---

[55] See Lord Bassam of Brighton, 'Citizenship', House of Lords debate, 28 November 2005, column 1.

efficiently pursued by other means the citizenship test can still have an important role to play but more of a symbolic kind.

The first issue to address is that there has been no public consultation since the test's launch in 2005. This has created an ever growing gap between public expectations and what the test delivers that is toxic to improving public confidence. More than two million tests sat later, it's time this requirement was officially reviewed to ensure it is fit for purpose, if it is to continue.

This review should be led by a new Citizenship Advisory Group, just as the first was. This body would be independent of government – like its original predecessor chaired by Crick. It would widely consult the public, critically examine how the test and its handbook can be designed around information citizens should have awareness about and which will further promote closer integration. Its members should come from across the mainstream political spectrum, but its aim focused on a non-partisan test of facts about history, government and history future-proofed against frequent change that is inclusive. The Group should remain in place after recommending a fourth edition test so that, as a cross-party Advisory Group, it can review the test contents annually to ensure their accuracy, ensuring it is aligned closely with public expectations and commands widespread confidence while aiding efforts to raise the profile of British citizenship generally. Never again should the test be mocked as a bad pub quiz that few citizens can pass.

This recommendation has broad support. The cross-party House of Lords Select Committee on Citizenship and Civic Participation noted the following in its 2018 report:

> Professor Brooks advocates a comprehensive, official review into the citizenship test. He points out that it is intended to enable and foster integration, yet there has been no review following any of the three editions published since 2005 into whether this has been achieved. 'The failure to consult, review and get feedback from

naturalised citizens who have undertaken and passed the process is alarming.' He suggests setting up an Advisory Group or Commission to look at the test. We see merit in this proposal. A small body which could examine what the test is seen to have achieved, both by those who have taken it and those who have not, would be in a good position to suggest how it might be improved.[56]

Nearly two decades later, such an official review is long overdue. The benefits are clear and deliverable. The public has little understanding, and even less confidence, about the test for British citizenship used in their name and to which they are a stakeholder.[57] It is essential that the public is involved, not a by-stander, which has done nothing to build public trust.[58] This can be corrected, and soon, with a test that can fulfil its original aims and purposes better than ever, in learning from past mistakes, building on where things have gone well and taking on board what has worked elsewhere like in the US.

The new fourth edition should not be a test whose aim is to make more people fail. If the policy goal is to exclude, this

[56] See House of Lords, *The Ties That Bind*, 117.
[57] On the idea of ethical citizenship and stakeholding, see Thom Brooks, 'Ethical citizenship and the stakeholder society' in Thom Brooks (ed), *Ethical Citizenship: British Idealism and the Politics of Recognition* (Basingstoke: Palgrave Macmillan, 2014): 125–138; Thom Brooks, 'The stakeholder society and the politics of hope', *Renewal* 23(1–2) (2015): 44–54; Thom Brooks, 'Labour can overcome its immigration problem', *Renewal* 24(4) (2016): 80–88; Thom Brooks, 'Saving multiculturalism with stakeholding: Hegel and the challenges of pluralism' in James Gledhill and Sebastian Stein (eds), *Hegel and Contemporary Practical Philosophy: Beyond Kantian Constructivism* (London: Routledge, 2020): 305–317; Thom Brooks, 'Cultivating citizenship: on the importance of stakeholding' in Thom Brooks (ed), *Political Emotions: Towards a Decent Public Sphere* (Basingstoke: Palgrave Macmillan, 2022): forthcoming.
[58] See Thom Brooks, 'Citizens' Conversations', *Fabian Review* 128(4) (2016): 24–25.

can be achieved more easily and transparently by other means. Retaining a trivial test is counterproductive where current citizens lack trust in it as they can't pass it either and those who do become resentful in having to overcome an unreasonable hurdle to remain. This point takes inspiration from both the working models in the US and now Australia, as well as the normative guidance from Carens, who notes:

> citizenship should be easily accessible as a matter of right to immigrants who want it after they have been in the country for a few years. That is largely compatible with tests of linguistic and civic knowledge, if the requirements for passing the tests are set at appropriately modest levels, so that most immigrants can pass the tests without difficulty. Reasonable tests of civic competence do not pose a substantial barrier to naturalization for most people.[59]

The state should provide opportunities, support and encouragement for prospective citizens to acquire this information.[60] This can be achieved in multiple ways, such as including information about the citizenship test in school education or launching a state-funded series of citizenship classes open to all where those seeking to learn more can meet other like-minded people and co-learn together. The latter echoes a recommendation in the original Advisory Group report that was not accepted. The key point to keep in mind is these individuals are those who are already members of our social community. The issue is not whether someone can be a part of the community where they already live or work, but whether to grant the status of citizenship, conferring its additional political and legal rights.[61]

---

[59] Carens, *The Ethics of Immigration*, 55.

[60] Ibid, 56.

[61] See ibid, 58.

It is contrary to the promotion of accountability and transparency that applicants are not supposed to know how well they did other than pass or fail.[62] This official response seems aimed at denying transparency, and as a result cannot be checked or challenged but merely accepted. But it's also noteworthy that this official reply by the current Immigration Minister isn't actually what happens for those like me going through the naturalization process. Contrary to what he has said, I was told my result when receiving in person my Indefinite Leave to Remain – and even congratulated by the border agent on my result. The agent noted that they could never pass the test, in yet another indictment of it. Everyone taking the test in future should know what parts of the test they got right – and which they got wrong. Applicants should not have to take the private test provider's word without any further feedback or information. This does not help secure confidence nor does it allow for accountability from the paying customers: specifically, those paying to sit the test

There is an issue around language. While the UK citizenship test can be taken in Welsh or Scots Gaelic, only *two* have ever tried to do it. We know one reported success of Brazilian immigrant Dr Rodolfo Piskorski who went public with his being the first to pass the citizenship test in Welsh.[63] The second to pass the test in a different language was a German national who sat the test in Scots Gaelic, but it is unconfirmed whether he or she passed.[64]

It is hardly any wonder this is so rare. While the test might be sat in English, Welsh or Scots Gaelic, the test handbook is only published in English. If it is to remain available in

---

[62] See Kevin Foster MP, 'British nationality: assessments', House of Commons debate, 5 February 2021, UIN 144731.

[63] See Katie Grant, 'Brazilian man becomes first person to pass British citizenship test in Welsh', *the i news* (4 October 2022).

[64] See Kevin Foster, 'British nationality: assessments', 5 February 2021, UIN 144730.

non-English languages, it is mandatory that the test handbook is published in these languages as well. And, if Welsh and Scots Gaelic tests will be available (and with their new test handbooks), the government must set a test (and test handbook) in Cornish. This is required in granting the Cornish protected minority status.

These additional versions of the test should be pursued. The test is about integration and playing an active role in a local community. English will usually be preferable, but not always. I have never been convinced that being fluent in Welsh cannot be best for integration where the majority speak Welsh in their everyday lives, for example.[65] It should be noted that, until October 2013, someone could pass the test in Welsh or Scots Gaelic and this would have proved sufficient knowledge in those languages exempting them from having to *also* prove English fluency. These languages were not seen as a problem for integration before and are not now either. These are British languages that are protected and promoted. There is cross-party support for this. Moreover, it remains unlikely that large numbers will avoid the test in English to take it in an alternative language anyway. In the amusing *How to Be a Brit*, George Mikes remarks, as a Hungarian living in Britain, that he thought he understood English until he heard the various different dialects which each had their own vocabulary like different species of English.[66] We should celebrate the diversity of Britain's dialects and languages. Leaving this out of test handbooks is only burying our heads in the sand. This can and should be put right.

I have not said much about what happens when you pass the test. Successful test takers are given a black and white form entitled 'Pass Notification Letter' that looks as ordinary as it sounds. Mine was slightly smudged fresh from a small

---

[65] See Brooks, *Becoming British*, 121–148.
[66] George Mikes, *How to Be a Brit* (Harmondsworth: Penguin, 1984): 27–31.

printer behind the test centre's desk. It would be a small, but welcome, effort to improve their appearance. Becoming British matters and passing a required citizenship test should be more than a tick box exercise – which the bland 'Pass Notification Letter' exemplifies. This should be freshened up by being a multicoloured, and more 'official' looking like a certificate and a document that prospective citizens will be proud to receive – not a print-off to merely stuff into an envelope with an application form uninterested if it is ever returned.

Crick's Life in the UK Advisory Group did not only recommend how to launch the citizenship test, but how to launch citizenship ceremonies that followed. If test reform has received little attention, citizenship ceremonies have fared even worse with no review since their start despite hundreds of thousands becoming naturalized at these events.

Citizenship ceremonies were introduced in the Nationality, Immigration and Asylum Act 2002, as was the citizenship test.[67] Crick's Group were tasked with setting out how tests and ceremonies might work. They started off with welcome fanfare – the first was held in Brent on 26 February 2004 attended by His Royal Highness Prince Charles and the then Home Secretary David Blunkett – but too rarely see anything like this since and almost never any media attention.[68]

The purpose of ceremonies was originally 'to make gaining British citizenship meaningful and celebratory rather than simply a bureaucratic process. New citizenship ceremonies will help people mark this important event'.[69] Former Home Secretary Charles Clarke told me that citizenship ceremonies "can be a very, very moving experience for new citizens".[70] He believed this was a good thing as becoming a British citizen

---

[67] See s3 and Schedule 1 of the Nationality, Immigration and Asylum Act 2002.

[68] BBC News, 'First citizenship ceremony for UK' (26 February 2004).

[69] David Blunkett quoted in Home Office, *First Edition*, 11.

[70] 'Interview with Charles Clarke', 29 September 2015.

should "be welcomed".[71] Clarke is absolutely right. These ceremonies are a welcome step forward that can, and should, be a heartwarming experience for new citizens.

The problem is the reality for many new citizens does not meet the original purpose behind the launch of the ceremonies. For example, the main part of most ceremonies are over in a matter of minutes held in more secluded settings. These are not events receiving notice or celebration outside the room, but minimalist affairs. While the national anthem is played, the words need not ever be learned. The occasion's main purpose is made clear in the letter of invitation that I received in 2011 for my citizenship ceremony:

> To complete the process of becoming a British citizen, you will need to attend a citizenship ceremony to receive your certificate. In the ceremony, you will take an oath or affirmation of allegiance to the Crown and a pledge of loyalty to the United Kingdom. This is a formal promise to Her Majesty the Queen and the United Kingdom.

While the event might take about an hour, the main ceremony of taking the oath, receipt of a naturalization certificate and receiving a small commemorative gift takes all of a few minutes.[72] Afterwards, there was pizza and juice available, but this was only for the local schoolchildren who came to sing two songs at my ceremony – 'The Candy Man Can' from *Willie Wonka and the Chocolate Factory* and 'The Bare Necessities' from *The Jungle Book* – which took up the largest share of the event.

A welcome letter from the Home Secretary reads awkwardly, slipping between referring to applicants as 'you' in the singular and 'your local communities' in the plural.[73] A former Home

---

[71] Ibid.

[72] These events were timetabled for 3.10 to 3.15pm at my citizenship ceremony, a mere five minutes. See Brooks, *Becoming British*, 47.

[73] Ibid, 48.

Secretary once confided in me that if these letters read impersonally it was because they were usually, if not always, written by a committee – and probably none would have experienced naturalization themselves and understood what is like to become British first-hand. Ceremonies should be a common experience run similarly from Land's End to John O'Groats and a moment of importance that can be done better. A first official review would go a very long way to ensuring citizenship ceremonies better fulfil their important purpose.

The cross-party House of Lords Select Committee on Citizenship and Civic Participation's 2018 report says:

> We were impressed by the ceremony itself and the way it was conducted; it plainly also impressed those taking part. But, as a number of witnesses have told us, these are very low key events. Professor Brooks wrote: 'Rarely is there any mention in the local or national press that citizenship ceremonies take place at all – and certainly a complete lack of political leadership in recognising and celebrating the achievement of new citizens. This is no way to treat or welcome new voters with full rights of citizenship into our shared community. It only seeks to alienate and push people apart.' … We agree that a case can be made for giving greater publicity to citizenship ceremonies. We believe that the group we recommend setting up to review the citizenship test should also seek feedback from those who have been involved in citizenship ceremonies, and consider how greater publicity and impact might be given to them.[74]

Like the original Crick-led Advisory Group, the House of Lords Select Committee accepts my recommendation that the profile of citizenship ceremonies must be raised and a newly

---

[74] See House of Lords, *The Ties That Bind*, 119.

constituted Group could complete this work in short order. I note further evidence given by Sadiq Khan, the Mayor of London, who recommend the UK considers having a similar event to the Australia Day where each year thousands of people make a pledge to their country and become Australian citizens. Khan remarked that such an event gives citizens old and new an opportunity to reflect on what it means to be an Australian citizen and 'celebrate the rights and the values they all share'.[75] Khan is right.

The government has paid no attention or interest to ensuring citizenship ceremonies achieve their aims and purposes. When asked what consultation had been undertaken with any of the two million new citizens naturalized through these ceremonies, the government admitted having nothing more than 'anecdotal evidence from those attending ceremonies … that they regard these as significant and symbolic events'.[76] In response to a question from Lord Kennedy of Southwark about what assessment has been made of the effect of citizenship ceremonies on promoting British values and improving integration, the official reply by Baroness Williams of Trafford was unequivocal: 'we have no plans to formally evaluate the impact of the ceremony'.[77] The government's unofficial moto appears to be 'do not look and you will not find'. This is unacceptable.

The political philosopher David Miller has claimed that 'new citizens should feel proud of what they have achieved, even if their original motive for seeking citizenship was instrumental'.[78] I agree, although he does not specify why they should. Moreover, this is – again – a one-way integrationist

---

[75] Ibid.

[76] See Baroness Williams of Trafford, 'British nationality: ceremonies', House of Lords debate, 11 October 2017, UIN HL1899.

[77] See Baroness William of Trafford, 'British nationality: ceremonies', House of Lords debate, 10 October 2017, UIN HL1845.

[78] Miller, *Strangers in Our Midst*, 139.

model where the pride is reserved only for the new citizen and does not extend to include the wider community of which the immigrant has become a new part. This only highlights the need for a public consultation led by an Advisory Group. Becoming British isn't something that happens only to new citizens, but to our community as we welcome new members. We all have a stake and should all have a say in ensuring we commemorate the achievements of becoming British in a fit for purpose way.

Sir Bernard Crick astutely observes that 'British citizenship is not a flag of convenience'.[79] Making the test more a bridge than barrier does not make it easy to become a citizen. The question is not whether there are hurdles to jump – there are many – but what role the test should play as a part of this bigger picture. The test has been best utilized where it is symbolic, inclusive, transparent and accessible. It lacks all these features now. A new Advisory Group setting out a fourth edition test can and should put this right.

---

[79] Bernard Crick, 'Introduction' in Home Office, *First Edition*, 13.

SEVEN

Conclusion and Recommendations

Over two million have sat the 'Life in the UK' citizenship test since its launch in 2005. Yet, there has never been any official review into whether it achieves its intended purpose and neither have citizens old or new been consulted in how the test might be improved. These are not reasons to abandon having the test and I believe it can have value, but this requires urgent and substantive reforms.

This book has detailed the many problems that have plagued the citizenship test since its rushed launch that has improved little over three editions. These problems should be no surprise to the government, with various reports and comment pieces calling them to action.[1] It will be over eight years since the last edition in 2013 and the longest stretch of an uncorrected, not updated test handbook in its history. Britain has left the European Union and the government is making a number of reforms to how the immigration system works. The time has never been better to review, refresh and relaunch the test to ensure it is fit for purpose and achieves its objectives. We should learn from the examples of citizenship tests abroad, but follow more closely the American example, as Australia has done already.

---

[1] For example, see Brooks, *The 'Life in the United Kingdom' Citizenship Test* and House of Lords Select Committee on Citizenship and Civic Participation, *The Ties That Bind*.

Kevin Foster MP, the current Immigration Minister, has said that 'when the Life in the UK handbook is next reviewed, the Home Office will consider all feedback on what should be covered in it'.[2] So, let me summarize 20 specific recommendations set across this book to inform how the next fourth edition of the test handbook should be refreshed, revised and relaunched:[3]

1. **A new Citizenship Advisory Group must be launched.** This should be a modest size including experts who have experienced naturalization first-hand. They should take inspiration from the original Life in the UK Advisory Group as an independent, non-partisan body to advise the government on the citizenship test and citizenship ceremonies.[4]

2. **The test handbook should state on its cover the date from which tests are based on its contents.** It must be clear from when the test handbook is the relevant text. Applicants should not be confused as to which available version is the source of information for their test.

3. **The test handbook should retain its reader-friendly format.** This includes accessible formats, including large print and braille.

4. **The test handbook should be fact-checked to correct errors.** This project should be informed by trying to reduce the overall number of facts deemed essential and looking at future-proofing test handbook content so it is less prone to change in the short term.

5. **The test handbook chapters should be redesigned.** There is a clear imbalance in size and content between

---

2   See Kevin Foster, 'British nationality: assessments', House of Commons debate, 21 October 2020, UIN 104188.

3   This list expands and develops earlier recommendations made in Brooks, 'The *Life in the UK* citizenship test', 58–60.

4   See Brooks, *Becoming British*, 276–282.

chapters not always matched by how much of their content appears in a test. The Advisory Group should strongly consider whether to require a mandatory score on questions about British values preventing anyone from passing the test if they fail too many questions about them.

6. **The test handbook should retain coverage of British history and culture.** This is a welcome addition to the materials tested since I called for its inclusion in 2011. But what is covered should be reconsidered in light of widespread criticisms and subject to a public consultation.

7. **The test handbook should make clear which, if any, historical dates should be memorized.** There are currently 278 historical dates listed in the third edition. Few, if any, need be recalled for any test. If this is for informational purposes only, this has a value and warrants mention. But if it is not essential for any test, this should be made clear.

8. **The test handbook should be revised to address gender, race and other relevant imbalances.** These imbalances are unnecessary and a serious problem. Britain is a diverse country that is proud of its diversity. This should be better reflected in the test handbook.

9. **The test handbook should include relevant information about the Cornish.** Since 2015, the Cornish are a protected minority group like the Welsh, Scots and Irish. They must be afforded equality. This entails inclusion of the Cornish flag, patron saint, language, regional food (Cornish pasty) and mention of famous Cornish individuals.

10. **The test handbook should be a complete resource for information about the test.** The handbook should include information about the test format, how many questions must be answered correctly to pass in addition to information that might be tested.

11. **The test handbook should include helpful information that need not be tested in an appendix clearly identified as not included in the test.** There is a value in including telephone numbers and websites for useful sources of relevant information. But the test must avoid any ambiguity over whether any of this material is tested.

12. **The test handbook should be freely available.** Integration is a two-way street. If the handbook contains information of importance for any citizen new or old, it should no longer be accessible only to those who can pay for it. It is also important that British citizens be able to freely access the test handbook.

13. **Any official supplemental texts, such as *Official Study Guide* and *Official Practice Questions*, should be published concurrently with the test handbook.** There is no good reason for delaying a group launch. This avoids giving advantages to some taking the test later than others who lacked access to such materials for sitting the same test.

14. **The test handbook and its supplemental texts should be consistent in content and format.** There should not be a different look or style between the official test handbook and its supplementary texts, as this may only confuse.

15. **The test handbook should be translated into Welsh and Scots Gaelic – and made available in Cornish.** The test is available in these languages. It is wrong that it cannot be studied in these languages first. As a protected minority, the Cornish language must be treated equally and this means a UK citizenship test in Cornish.

16. **There should be planned new editions every two to three years.** Instead of putting together a new edition once problems become too great with an existing edition, the Life in the UK Advisory Group can play a central role in regularly monitoring the test's content and performance.

17. **There should be official citizenship test classes available.** Their purpose is not to provide qualification, but support. Prospective citizens currently navigate the system, including gaining knowledge about life in the United Kingdom for the test, on their own. Becoming a citizen should not be left for individuals to do separately from the community they will join. There should be opportunities to meet others similarly situated to learn and support each other. Regular state-sponsored citizenship classes preferably run by someone who has naturalized can give the necessary support that has been missing. The original Advisory Group recommended a similar programme.

18. **The test should be seen as part of a larger strategy for improving integration.** The test should not be expected to ensure integration on its own. No memory test can do that. Its limited role should be considered within a wider strategy, rather than as a separate stream.

19. **The test's content should be taught in schools.** Schoolchildren need not pass the tests, but they should be aware of what is inside. This will help align the test content with public expectations about what information citizens should know.

20. **Citizenship ceremonies should be reviewed and refreshed.** Becoming British is a terrific achievement we should celebrate. The Advisory Group should review the purpose, use and delivery of ceremonies since their launch with an eye to ensure they gain greater publicity and impact.

If these reforms are enacted, the citizenship test could fulfil its original aims better than it ever has. Tests promoting integration and support inclusivity should act like a bridge for applicants to cross into citizenship. Using trick questions about non-essential information to exclude creates an inefficient and alienating barrier more easily achieved through other more transparent means, such as changing terms for qualifying residency period or achieving a minimum income threshold. The test as a bridge, not a barrier, is true to its original purpose to champion citizenship rather than put it further out of reach (and out of touch).[5]

In 2018, the House of Lords Select Committee on Citizenship and Civic Engagement published its report, *The Ties That Bind*, and quotes from my written evidence. It says:

> Professor Brooks was scathing in his criticism of the [test] book, stating: 'The test is regularly seen as the test for British citizenship that few British citizens can pass, with many migrants seeing it as an opportunity by the Home Office to extract increasingly more expensive fees through a test of random trivia meant to make more fail'. We agree. The current test seems to be, and to be regarded as, a barrier to acquiring citizenship rather than a means of creating better citizens.[6]

This unsatisfactory state of affairs need not continue. The government cannot pretend to ignore any longer these growing problems that they have been alerted to on multiple occasions.[7]

---

[5] See Elizabeth Meehan, 'Active citizenship: for integrating the immigrants' in Bernard Crick and Andrew Lockyer (eds), *Active Citizenship: What Could It Achieve and How?* (Edinburgh: Edinburgh University Press, 2010): 112–128, at 117.

[6] House of Lords Select Committee on Citizenship and Civic Participation, *The Ties That Bind*, 116 (para. 468).

[7] See Lord Taylor of Holbeach, 'Immigration: UK citizenship and nationality', House of Lords debate, 10 October 2013, column GC126 ('Although there has been some criticism, notably from Dr Thom Brooks at Durham, about that test') and Lord Parkinson of Whitley Bay, 'UK citizenship: history', House of Lords debate, 14 April 2021, column 1274 ('Professor Brooks … has certainly made his representations on the citizenship test well known').

We must act urgently to take up the recommendations outlined here to substantially update, refresh and improve the 'Life in the UK' test. Key to this task is recommitting ourselves to its original aims focused on integration and inclusivity, and reorienting its purpose to serving not as a *barrier*, but as a *bridge* to citizenship.

Appendix: Setting a New Citizenship Test

While I have set out several recommendations for how a new citizenship test might be refreshed and relaunched, there remains the issue of what this might look like, offering a concrete contrast with the past three test editions building from the analysis in the preceding chapters. Former Home Secretary Jacqui Smith pointed out to me that while 'the principle is right' about citizenship tests, it is difficult getting right the nitty-gritty of what multiple-choice questions and answers should be used.[1] I will attempt this task here.

As already noted, I believe the specific content should be driven from a public consultation – and this has not yet happened. So, I am not claiming that these sample test questions are *exactly* what I have in mind, but rather they are an *approximation* of the variety and complexity in mind. As a bridge, not a barrier, most of the hard work of qualifying is to be met by meeting various other requirements, such as residency tests, possessing 'good character' and sufficient knowledge of English among others.

The next text might separate its contents into 'Shared British values', 'British history and culture', 'British geography' and 'British government'. Some possible kinds of new test questions for a fourth edition might look like the following (answers **in bold**).

---

[1]   'Interview with Jacqui Smith', 28 September 2015.

Shared British values

1. Name TWO British values:
   A. Rule of law
   B. Not keeping dog on lead
   C. Fair play
   D. Driving on right-hand side of road

2. Everyone should be treated equally regardless of which TWO:
   A. Sexual orientation
   B. Disability
   C. Favourite food
   D. Hair colour

3. The initials 'NHS' stand for the:
   A. National Horse-riding Society
   B. Northumberland Helium Sales
   C. New Home Sales
   D. National Health Service

British history and culture

4. Who invaded England from Normandy in 1066 and later became King of England?
   A. Boudicca
   B. William the Conqueror
   C. Julius Caesar
   D. Robert the Bruce

5. The Kingdom of Great Britain began in 1707 bringing together which TWO nations:
   A. England
   B. Scotland
   C. Northern Ireland
   D. France

6. The Union Flag consists of the three overlapping crosses of St Andrew, St Patrick and who else:
   A. St Mark
   B. St Margaret
   C. St George
   D. St Pirin

7. Name TWO famous poets from Britain:
   A. William Shakespeare
   B. David Cameron
   C. Robert Burns
   D. Captain William Bligh

8. Britain's navy under Admiral Nelson defeated the fleets of France and Spain in which armed conflict:
   A. World War II
   B. Battle of Trafalgar
   C. Falkland Islands
   D. American Revolution

9. Florence Nightingale is the founder of modern:
   A. Nursing
   B. Chemistry
   C. Knitting
   D. Football

10. Which of the following was a famous suffragette campaigning for the rights of women to vote and stand for Parliament?
    A. Emmeline Pankhurst
    B. J.K. Rowling
    C. Shirley Bassey
    D. Paula Radcliffe

11. The UK's Prime Minister during the Second World War was:
    A. Earl Grey
    B. Winston Churchill
    C. Margaret Thatcher
    D. Tony Blair

12. Northern Ireland's Stormont Assembly was created by the:
    A. Good Friday Agreement
    B. Bayeux Tapestry
    C. War of the Roses
    D. Armistice Treaty

13. Christmas Day is:
    A. 1 January
    B. 14 February
    C. 1 April
    D. 25 December

14. Remembrance Day is:
    A. 14 February
    B. 31 October
    C. 5 November
    D. 11 November

15. England won the World Cup in:
    A. 1066
    B. 1945
    C. 1966
    D. 2000

16. One of Britain's most famous visual arts awards is:
    A. BAFTA
    B. The Turner Prize
    C. Comic Relief
    D. Duke of Edinburgh Award

17. Cornwall is famous for its:
    A. Pasty
    B. Pasta
    C. Haggis
    D. Yorkshire pudding

British geography

18. The capital of the United Kingdom is:
    A. London
    B. Birmingham
    C. Belfast
    D. Glasgow

19. Which nation is furthest north?
    A. Wales
    B. Scotland
    C. Northern Ireland
    D. Isle of Man

20. The patron saint of Wales is:
    A. St David
    B. St Patrick
    C. St Pirin
    D. St Andrew

21. Which TWO are UNESCO World Heritage sites:
    A. BBC Broadcasting House
    B. Wembley Stadium
    C. Stonehenge
    D. Hadrian's Wall

22. Scouse is the dialect associated with:
    A. Belfast
    B. Cardiff

C. Liverpool

D. Nottingham

British government

23. The UK's head of state is:
   A. Her Majesty the Queen
   B. The Prime Minister
   C. The Archbishop of Canterbury
   D. His Royal Highness The Prince of Wales

24. The head of the government is:
   A. The Leader of the Opposition
   B. The Chancellor of the Exchequer
   C. The Prime Minister
   D. The Home Secretary

25. The TWO Houses of Parliament are:
   A. House of Commons
   B. House of Lords
   C. House of York
   D. Housesteads

26. Which does NOT have a regional assembly or government?
   A. Scotland
   B. Wales
   C. Tyne and Wear
   D. Northern Ireland

27. Most people can stand for elected political office if they are BOTH:
   A. 18 or older
   B. University educated
   C. A British citizen
   D. Have family connections

28. It is a crime to:
   A. Harass someone because of their religion or ethnic origin
   B. Dislike football
   C. Walk a dog
   D. Avoid religious observances

29. If you have questions about tax, you should contact:
   A. Home Office
   B. HM Revenue & Customs (HMRC)
   C. Your family
   D. Your friends

30. The United Kingdom is part of a global 54 member state:
   A. Sports competition
   B. Art festival
   C. Commonwealth
   D. European Union

References

Parliamentary debates

Lord Bassam of Brighton, 'Citizenship', House of Lords debate, 28 November 2005, column 1.

Lord Blunkett, 'Integrated communities', House of Lords debate, 15 March 2018, column 1776.

Lord Blunkett, 'British citizenship', House of Lords debate, 3 October 2019, column 1779.

Lord Blunkett, 'Life in the UK test', House of Lords debate, 3 November 2020, column 628.

Lord Bourne of Aberystwyth, 'Integrated communities', House of Lords debate, 15 March 2018, column 1776.

Brokenshire, James, 'British nationality: assessments', House of Commons debate, 24 November 2014, UIN 215126.

Brokenshire, James, 'British nationality: assessments', House of Commons debate, 2 July 2015, UIN 3777.

Buchanan, George, 'Home Office', House of Commons debate, 16 July 1935, column 995.

Byrne, Liam, 'British nationality: assessments', House of Commons debate, 18 June 2008, column 961.

Clegg, Nick, 'Naturalisation test', House of Commons debate, 16 April 2007, column 470.

Clegg, Nick, 'Naturalisation test', House of Commons debate, 20 April 2007, column 830.

Lord Dubs, 'British citizenship', House of Lords debate, 3 October 2019, column 1778.

Foster, Kevin, 'British nationality: assessments', House of Commons debate, 3 March 2020, UIN 20526.

Foster, Kevin, 'British nationality: assessments', House of Commons debate, 21 June 2020, UIN 73099.

Foster, Kevin, 'British nationality: assessments', House of Commons debate, 21 July 2020, UIN 73098.

Foster, Kevin, 'British nationality: assessments', House of Commons debate, 15 October 2020, UIN 102176.

Foster, Kevin, 'British nationality: assessments', House of Commons debate, 21 October 2020, UIN 104188.

Foster, Kevin, 'British nationality: assessments', House of Commons debate, 5 February 2021, UIN 144730.

Foster, Kevin, 'British nationality: assessments', House of Commons debate, 5 February 2021, UIN 144731.

Foster, Kevin, 'British nationality: assessments', House of Commons debate, 8 February 2021, UIN 144733.

Baroness Gardner of Parkes, 'Citizenship test – question', House of Lords debate, 26 February 2013, column 955.

Green, Damian, 'Clause 39', House of Commons debate, 11 June 2009, column 78.

Green, Damian, 'British nationality', House of Commons debate, 22 November 2011, column 248.

Green, Damian, 'British nationality: assessments', House of Commons debate, 25 June 2012, column 29.

Lord Henley, 'British citizenship', House of Lords debate, 31 July 2012, column 0.

House of Lords, 'UK citizenship: history', House of Lords debate, 14 April 2021, columns 1272–1275.

Lynch, Holly and Kevin Foster, 'British nationality: assessments', Question for the Home Office, UIN 144730, tabled 27 January 2021.

May, Theresa, House of Commons debate, 25 March 2013, column 1277.

Onwurah, Chi and Damian Green, 'British nationality: assessments', House of Commons debate, 5 September 2012, column 350.

Lord Parkinson of Whitley Bay, 'UK citizenship: history', House of Lords debate, 14 April 2021, column 1274.

Lord Roberts of Llandudno, House of Lords debate, 4 July 2013, column 1397.

Baroness Scotland of Asthal, 'Citizenship', House of Lords debate, 22 November 2005, column 200.

Lord Singh of Wimbledon, 'Life in the UK test', House of Lords debate, 3 November 2020, 628.

Lord Taylor of Holbeach, 'British citizenship', House of Lords debate, 25 February 2013, column 198.

Lord Taylor of Holbeach, 'Citizenship test – question', House of Lords debate, 26 February 2013, column 954.

Lord Taylor of Holbeach, 'Citizenship test – question', House of Lords debate, 26 February 2013, column 955.

Lord Taylor of Holbeach, 'British citizenship', House of Lords debate, 22 April 2013, column 354.

Lord Taylor of Holbeach, 'British citizenship', House of Lords debate, 21 May 2013, column 44.

Lord Taylor of Holbeach, 'British citizenship', House of Lords debate, 23 May 2013, column 44.

Lord Taylor of Holbeach, 'Immigration: UK citizenship and nationality', House of Lords debate, 10 October 2013, column GC127.

Lord Taylor of Holbeach, 'Immigration: UK citizenship and nationality', House of Lords debate, 10 October 2013, column GC128.

Baroness Williams of Trafford, 'British nationality: assessments', House of Lords debate, 9 October 2017, UIN HL1746.

Baroness Williams of Trafford, 'British nationality: assessments', House of Lords debate, 9 October 2017, UIN HL1747.

Baroness Williams of Trafford, 'British nationality: ceremonies', House of Lords debate, 10 October 2017, UIN HL1845.

Baroness Williams of Trafford, 'British nationality: ceremonies', House of Lords debate, 11 October 2017, UIN HL1899.

Baroness Williams of Trafford, 'British nationality: assessments', House of Lords debate, 23 October 2017, UIN HL1747.

Baroness Williams of Trafford, 'British nationality: assessments', House of Lords debate, 23 October 2017, UNIN HL1793.

Baroness Williams of Trafford, 'British nationality: assessments', House of Lords debate, 23 October 2017, UIN HL1794.

Baroness Williams of Trafford, 'British nationality: assessments', House of Lords debate, 24 October 2017, UIN HL1872.

Baroness Williams of Trafford, 'British citizenship', House of Lords debate, 3 October 2019, column 1780.

Baroness Williams of Trafford, 'British nationality: assessments', House of Lords debate, 29 March 2019, UIN HL14599.

Baroness Williams of Trafford, 'British nationality: assessments', House of Lords debate, 7 December 2020, UIN HL10607.

Printed sources

Akehurst, Nathan, 'Why Labour must be the party of migration justice', *Renewal* 27(4) (2019): 23–34.

Anderson, Bridget, *Us and Them: The Dangerous Politics of Immigration Control*. Oxford: Oxford University Press, 2013.

Australian Citizenship Council, *Australian Citizenship for a New Century*. Canberra: Australian Citizenship Council, 2000.

Australian Government, *Australian Citizenship … A Common Bond: Government Response to the Report of the Australian Citizenship Council*. Canberra: Commonwealth of Australia, 2001.

Balibar, Etienne, *Citizenship*. Cambridge: Polity, 2015.

Bertram, Christopher, *Do States Have the Right to Exclude Immigrants?* Cambridge: Polity, 2018.

Blunkett, David, 'Preface' in Home Office, *Life in the United Kingdom: A Journey to Citizenship*. London: The Stationery Office, 2005, p 4.

British Future, *Barriers to Britishness: Report of the Alberto Costa Inquiry into Citizenship Policy*. London: British Future, 2020.

Brock, Gillian, *Migration and Political Theory*. Cambridge: Polity, 2021.

Brooks, Thom, 'The British citizenship test: the case for reform', *Political Quarterly* 83(3) (2012): 560–566.

Brooks, Thom, 'Citizenship' in Hugh LaFollette (ed), *The International Encyclopedia of Ethics*. Oxford: Blackwell, 2013, pp 764–773.

Brooks, Thom, 'Ethical citizenship and the stakeholder society' in Thom Brooks (ed), *Ethical Citizenship: British Idealism and the Politics of Recognition*. Basingstoke: Palgrave Macmillan, 2014, pp 125–138.

Brooks, Thom, 'The stakeholder society and the politics of hope', *Renewal* 23(1–2) (2015): 44–54.

Brooks, Thom, *Becoming British: UK Citizenship Examined*. London: Biteback, 2016.

Brooks, Thom, 'Citizens' conversations', *Fabian Review* 128(4) (2016): 24–25.

Brooks, Thom, 'Labour can overcome its immigration problem', *Renewal* 24(4) (2016): 80–88.

Brooks, Thom, 'Testing times for citizenship', *Centre Wright* (Summer 2016): 32.

Brooks, Thom, 'The *Life in the UK* citizenship test and the urgent need for its reform' in Devyani Prabhat (ed), *Citizenship in Times of Turmoil? Theory, Practice and Policy*. London: Edward Elgar, 2019, pp 22–60.

Brooks, Thom, 'Saving multiculturalism with stakeholding: Hegel and the challenges of pluralism' in James Gledhill and Sebastian Stein (eds), *Hegel and Contemporary Practical Philosophy: Beyond Kantian Constructivism*. London: Routledge, 2020, pp 305–317.

Brooks, Thom, 'Cultivating citizenship: on the importance of stakeholding' in Thom Brooks (ed), *Political Emotions: Towards a Decent Public Sphere*. Basingstoke: Palgrave Macmillan, 2022.

Brooks, Thom, *The Trust Factor: Essays on the Current Political Crisis and Hope for the Future*. London: Methuen, 2022.

Byrne, Bridget, 'Testing times: the place of the citizenship test in the UK immigration regime and new citizens' responses to it', *Sociology* 51(2) (2017): 323–338.

Byrne, Liam, *A More United Kingdom*. London: Demos, 2008.

Carens, Joseph H., *The Ethics of Immigration*. Oxford: Oxford University Press, 2013.

Castelino, Celine, *Pass the New Life in the UK Test*, ed. Chris Taylor. London: National Institute of Adult Continuing Education, 2013.

Cooke, Melanie, 'Barrier or entitlement? The language and citizenship agenda in the United Kingdom', *Language Assessment Quarterly* 6(1) (2009): 71–77.

Crick, Bernard, 'Identity politics' in Bernard Crick and Andrew Lockyer (eds), *Active Citizenship: What Could It Achieve and How?* Edinburgh: Edinburgh University Press, 2010, p 193.

de Waal, Tamar, *Integration Requirements for Immigrants in Europe: A Legal-Philosophical Inquiry*. Oxford: Hart, 2021.

Edmonds, W. Alex and Thomas D. Kennedy, *An Applied Guide to Research Designs: Quantitative, Qualitative and Mixed Methods, 2nd edition*. Thousand Oaks: SAGE, 2017.

Farer, Tom, *Migration and Integration: The Case for Liberalism with Borders*. Cambridge: Cambridge University Press, 2020.

Fox, Kate, *Watching the English: The Hidden Rules of English Behaviour*. London: Hodder, 2004.

Goodhart, David, *The British Dream: Successes and Failures of Post-War Immigration*. London: Atlantic Books, 2013.

Goodman, Sara Wallace, *Immigration and Membership Politics in Western Europe*. Cambridge: Cambridge University Press, 2014.

Hampshire, James, *The Politics of Immigration*. London: Routledge, 2013.

Hirsch, Afua, *Brit(ish): On Race, Identity and Belonging*. London: Jonathan Cape, 2018.

Home Office, *Building Cohesive Communities: A Report of the Ministerial Group on Public Order and Community Cohesion*. London: Home Office, 2001.

Home Office, *The New and the Old: The Report of the 'Life in the United Kingdom' Advisory Group*. London: Home Office Communication Directorate, 2003.

Home Office, *Life in the United Kingdom: A Journey to Citizenship*. London: The Stationery Office, 2005.

Home Office, *Life in the United Kingdom: A Journey to Citizenship, 2nd edition*. London: The Stationery Office, 2007.

Home Office, *Official Citizenship Test Study Guide*. London: The Stationery Office, 2007.

Home Office, *Life in the United Kingdom: A Guide for New Residents, 3rd edition*. London: The Stationery Office, 2013.

Home Office, *A Practical Guide to Living in the United Kingdom*. London: The Stationery Office (TSO), 2014.

House of Lords Select Committee on Citizenship and Civic Engagement, *The Ties That Bind: Citizenship and Civic Engagement in the 21st Century*. London: House of Lords, 2018 (HL Paper 118).

Jarvis, Lee, Lee Marsden and Eylem Atakav, 'Public conceptions and constructions of "British values": a qualitative analysis', *British Journal of Politics and International Relations* 22(1) (2020): 85–101.

Johnston, Neil, *Constituency Boundary Reviews and the Number of MPs*, House of Commons Library. London: Parliament, 8 June 2021.

Joppke, Christian, *Citizenship and Immigration*. Cambridge: Polity, 2010.

Kafka, Franz, *The Trial*, trans. Willa and Edwin Muir. New York: Schocken Books, 1992.

Kiwan, Dina, 'A journey to citizenship in the United Kingdom', *International Journal on Multicultural Societies* 10(1) (2008): 60–75.

Kiwan, Dina, 'Active citizenship, multiculturalism and mutual understanding' in Bernard Crick and Andrew Lockyer (eds), *Active Citizenship: What Could It Achieve and How?* Edinburgh: Edinburgh University Press, 2010, pp 100–111.

Kymlicka, Will, *Multicultural Odysseys: Navigating the New International Politics of Diversity*. Oxford: Oxford University Press, 2007.

Meehan, Elizabeth, 'Active citizenship: for integrating the immigrants' in Bernard Crick and Andrew Lockyer (eds), *Active Citizenship: What Could It Achieve and How?* Edinburgh: Edinburgh University Press, 2010, pp 112–128.

Mikes, George, *How to Be a Brit*. Harmondsworth: Penguin, 1984.

Miller, David, *Strangers in Our Midst: The Political Philosophy of Immigration*. Cambridge, MA: Harvard University Press, 2016.

Mitchell, Michael, *Life in the United Kingdom: Official Practice Questions and Answers*. London: The Stationery Office, 2013.

Morrice, Linda, 'British citizenship, gender and migration: the containment of cultural differences and the stratification of belonging', *British Journal of Sociology of Education* 38(5) (2017): 597–609.

Osler, Audrey, 'Testing citizenship and allegiance: policy, politics and the education of adult migrants in the UK', *Education, Citizenship and Social Justice* 4(1) (2009): 63–79.

Parekh, Bhikhu (ed), *The Future of Multi-Ethnic Britain: Report of the Commission on the Future of Multi-Ethnic Britain*. London: Profile, 2000.

Parekh, Bhikhu, *Rethinking Multiculturalism: Cultural Diversity and Political Theory*. Basingstoke: Palgrave Macmillan, 2006.

Patten, Alan, *The Moral Foundations of Minority Rights*. Princeton: Princeton University Press, 2014.

Phillips, Anne, *Multiculturalism without Culture*. Princeton: Princeton University Press, 2007.

Portes, Jonathan, *What Do We Know and What Should We Do About Immigration?* Thousand Oaks: SAGE, 2019.

Prabhat, Devyani, *Britishness, Belonging and Citizenship: Experiencing Nationality Law*. Bristol: Policy Press, 2018.

Ratcliffe, Peter and Ines Newman (eds), *Promoting Social Cohesion: Implications for Policy and Evaluation*. Bristol: Policy Press, 2011.

Red Squirrel Publishing, *Life in the UK Test Study Guide: 2020 Edition*. London: Red Squirrel Publishing, 2020.

Rimmer, Sue Harris, *Bills Digest: Australian Citizenship Amendment (Citizenship Testing) Bill 2007*, Parliamentary Library. Canberra: Australian Parliament, 2007.

Rutter, Jill, *Moving Up and Getting On: Migration, Integration and Social Cohesion in the UK*. Bristol: Policy Press, 2015.

Sager, Alex (ed), *The Ethics and Politics of Immigration: Core Issues and Emerging Trends*. London: Rowman & Littlefield, 2016.

Sales, Rosemary, *Understanding Immigration and Refugee Policy: Contradictions and Continuities*. Bristol: Policy Press, 2007.

Scottish Government, *Scotland's Future: Your Guide to an Independent Scotland*. Edinburgh: Scottish Government, 2013.

Spencer, Sarah, *The Migration Debate*. Bristol: Policy Press, 2011.

Spiro, Peter J., *Beyond Citizenship: American Identity After Globalization*. Oxford: Oxford University Press, 2008.

Stagg, Helen R., Jane Jones, Graham Bickler and Ibrahim Abubakar, 'Poor uptake of primary healthcare registration among recent entrants to the UK: a retrospective cohort study', *British Medical Journal Open* (2012), doi:10.1136/bmjopen-2012-001453.

Steventon, Adam and Martin Bardsley, 'Use of secondary care in England by international immigrants', *Journal of Health Services Research and Policy* 16(2) (2011): 90–94.

Taylor, Chris *ESOL and Citizenship: A Teacher's Guide*. Leicester: NIACE, 2007.

Uberoi, Elise and Neil Johnston, 'Constituency boundary reviews and the number of MPs', House of Commons Library. London: House of Commons, 8 June 2021.

van Oers, Ricky, *Deserving Citizenship: Citizenship Tests in Germany, the Netherlands and the United Kingdom*. Leiden: Martinus Nijhoff Publishers, 2013.

Wales, Jenny, *Citizenship Today – Student's Book: Endorsed by Edexcel, 3rd edition*. London: Collins, 2009.

Wales, Jenny, *Collins Revisions – GCSE Citizenship for Edexcel*. London: Collins, 2010.

Wales, Jenny, *Life in the United Kingdom: Official Study Guide*. London: The Stationery Office, 2013.

Yeo, Colin, *Welcome to Britain: Fixing Our Broken Immigration System*. London: Biteback, 2020.

Online sources

ABC News, 'Don gets dropped from citizenship test' (21 November 2008), https://www.abc.net.au/news/2008-11-22/don-gets-dropped-from-citizenship-test/214836

Australian Government, *Australian Citizenship: Much More Than a Ceremony*, Canberra: Department of Immigration and Multicultural Affairs, 2006, http://nla.gov.au/nla.arc-64133

Barr, Sabrina, 'Why does the queen have two birthdays?' *The Independent* (12 June 2021), https://www.independent.co.uk/life-style/royal-family/how-old-is-queen-elizabeth-b1864598.html

BBC News, 'Churchill votes greatest Briton' (24 November 2002), http://news.bbc.co.uk/1/hi/entertainment/2509465.stm

BBC News, 'First citizenship ceremony for UK' (26 February 2004), http://news.bbc.co.uk/1/hi/uk_politics/3487892.stm

BBC News, 'Curry house founder is honoured' (29 September 2005), http://news.bbc.co.uk/1/hi/england/london/4290124.stm

BBC News, 'New UK citizenship testing starts' (1 November 2005), http://news.bbc.co.uk/1/hi/uk_politics/4391710.stm

BBC News, 'The nation's favourite poet result' (14 May 2009), https://www.bbc.co.uk/poetryseason/vote_results.shtml

BBC News, 'British citizenship test: one in three immigrants fails' (27 May 2010), http://news.bbc.co.uk/1/hi/8707152.stm

BBC News, 'Jersey States rejects citizenship test for non-British election candidates' (11 February 2021), https://www.bbc.co.uk/news/world-europe-jersey-56008244.

BBC Radio 4, 'You and yours' (10 October 2011), http://www.bbc.co.uk/iplayer/episode/b015mzl2/You_and_Yours_Chris_Tarrant_on_dramatic_pauses/

Beamish, Sam, 'People urged to write Cornish as their nationality in census after tick box snub', *Cornwall Live* (3 March 2021), https://www.cornwalllive.com/news/cornwall-news/people-urged-write-cornish-nationality-5039056

Blackstock, Gordon, 'Scots immigrants left confused as UK citizenship test app gives incorrect answers', *Daily Record* (21 March 2021), https://www.dailyrecord.co.uk/news/scottish-news/scots-immigrants-left-confused-uk-23765836

Blair, Tony, 'Tony Blair's Britain speech', *The Guardian* (28 March 2000), https://www.theguardian.com/uk/2000/mar/28/britishidentity.tonyblair

Brooks, Thom, *The 'Life in the United Kingdom' Citizenship Test: Is It Unfit for Purpose?* (Durham: Durham University, 2013), https://papers.ssrn.com/sol3/papers.cfm?abstract_id=2280329

Brooks, Thom, 'The "Life in the UK" citizenship test: is it unfit for purpose?', Durham University, YouTube (18 June 2013), https://www.youtube.com/watch?v=RhSZuzCvOB4

Brooks, Thom, 'The "Life in the UK" test has morphed into a barrier to immigration', *New Statesman* (16 July 2013), http://www.newstatesman.com/politics/2013/07/life-uk-test-has-morphed-barrier-immigration

Brooks, Thom, 'Cornish pasties must be added to the UK citizenship test', *The Conversation* (25 April 2014), https://theconversation.com/cornish-pasties-must-be-added-to-the-uk-citizenship-test-25970

Brooks, Thom, *A Practical Guide to Living in the United Kingdom: A Report* (Durham: Durham University, 2015), https://papers.ssrn.com/sol3/papers.cfm?abstract_id=2622908

Brooks, Thom, 'Good luck with the citizenship test, Meghan Markle. It's a mess', *The Guardian* (1 March 2018), https://www.theguardian.com/commentisfree/2018/mar/01/british-citizenship-test-meghan-markle-brexit-reform

Brooks, Thom, 'Sajid Javid is right – the British citizenship test is like a bad pub quiz. So what is he going to do about it?' *The Independent* (3 October 2018), https://www.independent.co.uk/voices/sajid-javid-conservative-party-conference-speech-british-citizenship-test-pub-quiz-a8566186.html

Brooks, Thom, 'The UK citizenship test is closer to a bad pub quiz than a rite of passage. It has to be re-written', *The Independent* (25 August 2020), https://www.independent.co.uk/voices/home-office-uk-british-citizenship-test-history-slavery-empire-a9685851.html

Cameron, David, 'Prime minister's speech on immigration' (10 October 2011), https://www.gov.uk/government/speeches/prime-ministers-speech-on-immigration

CBS News, 'Most Americans could not pass a citizenship test, a major issue for the country' (19 January 2021), https://www.cbsnews.com/video/most-americans-could-not-pass-a-citizenship-test-a-major-issue-for-the-country/

Coats, Matthew, 'Letter' (11 July 2008), https://www.whatdotheyknow.com/request/14965/response/52373/attach/html/5/20080717%20ABNI%20future.doc.html.

Coughlan, Sean, 'The symbolic target of 50% at university reached', BBC News (26 September 2019), https://www.bbc.co.uk/news/education-49841620

Council of Europe, 'Framework Convention for the Protection of National Minorities', https://www.coe.int/en/web/conventions/full-list?module=treaty-detail&treatynum=157

Creed, Rebecca, 'Essex University: two thirds would not pass UK citizenship test', *Daily Gazette* (9 January 2021), https://www.gazette-news.co.uk/news/18993710.essex-university-two-thirds-not-pass-uk-citizenship-test/

Crown Prosecution Service, 'Non-jury trials' (November 2019), https://www.cps.gov.uk/legal-guidance/non-jury-trials

Department of Home Affairs (Australian Government), *Citizenship Interview and Test* (2021), https://immi.homeaffairs.gov.au/citizenship/test-and-interview/our-common-bond

Dutch Ministry of Justice and Security, *Civic Integration for More Secure Residence Permit and Naturalization* (2022), https://ind.nl/en/Pages/Integration-in-the-netherlands.aspx

Easton, Mark, 'Define Britishness? It's like painting wind', BBC News (2 March 2012), http://www.bbc.co.uk/news/uk-17218635

Edgar, David, 'The British history new citizens must learn: no radicals, no homosexuals, no holocaust', *The Guardian* (11 March 2013), https://www.theguardian.com/commentisfree/2013/mar/11/battle-britain-history-new-uk-citizens

French Government, 'Naturalisation' (2022), https://www.service-public.fr/particuliers/vosdroits/F2213

French Ministry de l'Interieur, *Livret du Citoyen* (2015), https://www.immigration.interieur.gouv.fr/content/download/79473/584355/file/Livret-du-citoyen_pageapage_5mars2015.pdf

German Federal Ministry of the Interior and Community, *Naturalisation* (2022), https://www.bmi.bund.de/EN/topics/migration/naturalization/naturalization-node.html

Glendinning, Lee, 'Citizenship guide fails its history exam', *The Guardian* (29 April 2006), https://www.theguardian.com/uk/2006/apr/29/immigration.immigrationpolicy

Grant, Katie, 'Brazilian man becomes first person to pass British citizenship test in Welsh', *the i news* (4 October 2022), https://inews.co.uk/news/wales-brazilian-british-citizenship-test-welsh-language-676945

Hall, Macer, 'Now Michael Gove wants pupils aged five to learn poetry', *Daily Express* (11 June 2012), https://www.express.co.uk/news/uk/325796/Now-Michael-Gove-wants-pupils-aged-five-to-learn-poetry

Hallett, Emma, 'Will minority status help Cornwall?', BBC News (24 April 2014), https://www.bbc.co.uk/news/uk-england-27139692

Historical Association, 'Britain first: the official history of the United Kingdom according to the Home Office – a critical review' (11 September 2020), https://historyjournal.org.uk/2020/09/11/britain-first-the-official-history-of-the-united-kingdom-according-to-the-home-office-a-critical-review/

HM Government, 'Knowledge of language and life in the UK exemption: long term physical or mental condition' (2016), https://www.gov.uk/government/publications/life-in-the-uk-test-exemption-long-term-physical-or-mental-condition

HM Government, 'Life in the UK test' (2022), https://www.gov.uk/life-in-the-uk-test

HM Ministry of Housing, 'New funding to preserve Cornish culture, language and heritage' (5 July 2019), https://www.gov.uk/government/news/new-funding-to-preserve-cornish-culture-language-and-heritage

HM Treasury, 'Cornish granted minority status within the UK' (24 April 2014), https://www.gov.uk/government/news/cornish-granted-minority-status-within-the-uk

The Independent, 'Rudyard Kipling's "If" voted nation's favourite poem' (13 October 1995), https://www.independent.co.uk/news/rudyard-kipling-s-if-voted-nation-s-favourite-poem-1577258.html

Kwok, Abe, 'In the end, Trump's tougher citizenship test had no impact on immigrants', *Arizona Republic* (14 June 2021), https://eu.azcentral.com/story/opinion/op-ed/abekwok/2021/06/14/trump-citizenship-test-no-impact-immigrants-scored-higher/7661722002/

learndirect, 'Company history' (2022), https://www.learndirect.com/about-us/company-history

Meikle, James, 'Michael Gove in clash over free schools freedom of information requests', *The Guardian* (20 February 2013), https://www.theguardian.com/education/2013/feb/20/michael-gove-clash-free-schools

Mock the Week, 'The British citizenship test is like a bad pub quiz (and so is Mock the Week)', BBC 2 (10 January 2019), https://www.youtube.com/watch?v=xeCFPw6ah8Y

National Health Service, 'Improving GP registration among socially excluded groups' (2010), https://www.google.co.uk/url?sa=t&rct=j&q=&esrc=s&source=web&cd=&ved=2ahUKEwinseapnt_1AhXBoFwKHXbGDloQFnoECAUQAQ&url=https%3A%2F%2Fwww.bl.uk%2Fbritishlibrary%2F~%2Fmedia%2Fbl%2Fglobal%2Fsocial-welfare%2Fpdfs%2Fnon-secure%2Fi%2Fn%2Fc%2Finclusion-health-improving-primary-care-for-socially-excluded-people.pdf&usg=AOvVaw1nXeOafEcSOOuqvnpGIU-U

News.com.au, 'Don Bradman was never in Australian citizenship test' (21 October 2009), https://www.news.com.au/breaking-news/citizenship-test-doesnt-include-don-bradman/news-story/5bed847c37a8f5cc8844fce6e9bcf695)

Office for National Statistics, *2011 Census*, https://www.ons.gov.uk/census/2011census

Office for National Statistics, *Overview of the UK Population: January 2021* (14 January 2021), https://www.ons.gov.uk/peoplepopulationandcommunity/populationandmigration/populationestimates/articles/overviewoftheukpopulation/january2021

O'Hagan, Andrew, 'A journey to citizenship', *London Review of Books*, 28(23) (30 November 2006), https://www.lrb.co.uk/the-paper/v28/n22/andrew-o-hagan/short-cuts

Parkinson, Justin, 'British citizenship test "like bad pub quiz"', BBC News (13 June 2013), https://www.bbc.co.uk/news/uk-politics-22892444

Press Association, 'Citizenship test has become a bad pub quiz, says academic', *The Guardian* (14 June 2013), https://www.theguardian.com/uk/2013/jun/14/citizenship-test-pub-quiz

PSI e-Assessment, 'Terms and conditions for booking and taking the Life in the UK test' (2022), LitUK_Ts_and_Cs_Added_Value_v1.0.pdf (lituktestbooking.co.uk)

Rachwani, Mostafa, 'The new Australian citizenship test: what is it and what has changed?' *The Guardian* (17 September 2020), https://www.theguardian.com/australia-news/2020/sep/18/the-new-australian-citizenship-test-what-is-it-and-what-has-changed

Reuters, 'Strewth! Australia drops cricket from citizenship test' (22 November 2008), https://www.reuters.com/article/oukoe-uk-australia-citizenship/strewth-australia-drops-cricket-from-citizenship-test-idUKTRE4AL0BG20081122

Romero, Simon and Miriam Jordan, 'New U.S. citizenship test is longer and more difficult', *New York Times* (3 December 2020), https://www.nytimes.com/2020/12/03/us/citizenship-test.html

Runnymede Trust, 'Commission on the Future of Multi-Ethnic Britain' (2000), https://www.runnymedetrust.org/companies/29/74/Future-of-Multi-Ethnic-Britain-The.html

Ryan, Kerry, 'Citizenship by the booklet', *Inside Story* (5 March 2013), http://inside.org.au/citizenship-by-the-booklet

Sands, Geneva, 'Biden administration rolls back Trump-era citizenship civics test', *CNN* (22 February 2021), https://edition.cnn.com/2021/02/22/politics/biden-roll-back-trump-citizenship-test/index.html

Sippitt, Amy, 'Health tourists: how much do they cost and who pays?' *Full Fact* (13 April 2015), https://fullfact.org/health/health-tourism/

Smith, David Woodruff, 'Phenomenology', *Stanford Encyclopedia of Philosophy* (2013), https://plato.stanford.edu/entries/phenomenology/

Sukhadwala, Sejal, 'The story of London's first Indian restaurant', *Londinist* (January 2019), https://londonist.com/2016/06/the-story-of-london-s-first-indian-restaurant#:~:text=It%27s%20commonly%20assumed%20that%20London%27s,hundred%20years%20ago%2C%20in%201810.&text=He%20was%20also%20the%20first%20Indian%20to%20publish%20books%20in%20English

The Times, 'Half of grassroots Tories would abolish Supreme Court', *The Times* (10 October 2019), https://www.thetimes.co.uk/article/half-of-grassroots-tories-would-abolish-supreme-court-whgjwf3ls

Travis, Alan, 'UK migrants to face "patriotic" citizenship test', *The Guardian* (1 July 2012), https://www.theguardian.com/uk/2012/jul/01/uk-migrants-patriotic-citizenship-test

UK Visas and Immigration, 'Life in the UK test: identification documents' (2022), https://assets.publishing.service.gov.uk/government/uploads/system/uploads/attachment_data/file/1037459/LitUK_candidate_identification_requirements_v8.2.pdf

US Citizenship and Immigration Services, 'Study for the test (2008 version)', https://www.uscis.gov/citizenship/find-study-materials-and-resources/study-for-the-test

Watt, Nicholas, 'David Cameron flunks citizenship test on David Letterman's Late Show', *The Guardian* (27 September 2012), https://www.theguardian.com/politics/2012/sep/27/david-cameron-letterman-late-show

Wellman, Christopher Heath, 'Immigration', *Stanford Encyclopedia of Philosophy* (21 May 2019), https://plato.stanford.edu/entries/immigration/

Index

9 781529 218527